'For a very long time no\
has a major task in how :
men. The attendance figures at all ages show this concern. But there are issues for society as a whole: why are boys achieving less than girls in school? Why is crime more prevalent amongst men than women? And many other questions besides. So both society and the church should welcome the work being done to try to discover some answers to these questions.

Carolyn Edwards' book, clearly based on her research, is a really helpful addition to the growing literature on this issue. Shaping her findings around ten spiritual connections provides a valuable framework for outlining her findings and suggestions about actions that flow from them. Personally, I valued her willingness to ask hard questions of our extremely safety-conscious culture; I am sure she is right to challenge us to explore wise risk-taking. She highlights the importance and value of play emerging within several of the spiritual connections she identifies. This should not surprise her readers, though it will possibly surprise some. Play is an area of spirituality, including the very helpful section on humour, which needs to be investigated more fully. She wisely suggests that godly play is one way of exploring this, but equally wisely suggests that the exploration of play will need to be wider than this, and should include the place and role of computer gaming.

I am delighted to be able to commend this book. It actually offers helpful advice on working with girls as well – for Carolyn notes all the way through that the ten spiritual connections apply to them too. However, there is evidence of some differences in how boys and girls generally respond to these. Everyone working with children will gain from taking Carolyn's work seriously.'

The Right Reverend Paul Butler, Bishop of Southwell and Nottingham

'Men often dismiss church as irrelevant, because we fail to connect with them. To correct this trend, we need to start by looking at boys who grow up to be men. Boys are spiritual beings – but much of organized Christianity fails to understand what makes them tick.

Carolyn Edwards has undertaken some thoughtful research, and has come up with insightful and practical suggestions of ways to reconnect with boys. She is a practitioner, and that shows throughout the book, as ideas come across as tested and tried.

As the parents of four lively boys who are now grown men, we commend this book as extremely helpful and packed with good suggestions. As teachers involved in training people for leadership, we commend it as essential reading for any who are serious about engaging in the mission of God.'
Ian and Ruth Coffey, Director of Leadership Training, and Tutor in Pastoral Studies, respectively, at Moorlands College, Dorset

'*Slugs and Snails and Puppy Dogs' Tails* is a really useful, well-researched and powerful contribution to the increasing interest in how the church deals with boys and their needs. The realistic advice and practical suggestions here are underpinned by theological reading and wide references, making it a really helpful resource. This book is guaranteed to help children's workers and all those who want to see the church full of boys . . . and full of men in the future!'
Nick Harding, Children's Ministry Adviser and author of Boys, God and the Church

'An important contribution to the issue of boys' spirituality, taking it from theoretical research, which the author is well qualified to offer, to well-grounded practical application, based on her many years of experience as a children's worker. Boys

especially need their advocates at the present time. Carolyn Edwards offers them another supporting voice.'
Ian White, Programme Leader, Children's and Youth Ministry courses, Cliff College

'For those of us who have a heart to connect with children and young people, *Slugs and Snails and Puppy Dogs' Tails* will be an invaluable resource. Down-to-earth and highly readable, Carolyn's findings are drawn from quality research and years of experience working with children in a range of settings. She communicates with insight, clarity and humour, and provides highly practical suggestions for positive approaches to assisting boys in developing spiritually. The practical wisdom in this book has a broader application to work with children and young people, and I will be recommending it wholeheartedly to students, children's and youth workers, ministers, teachers and parents alike.'
Jo Whitehead, Assistant Director, Midlands Centre for Youth Ministry

ivp

Carolyn Edwards

slugs & snails & puppy dogs' tails

Helping boys connect with God

INTER-VARSITY PRESS
Norton Street, Nottingham NG7 3HR, England
Email: ivp@ivpbooks.com
Website: www.ivpbooks.com

First published 2011

British Library Cataloguing in Publication Data
A catalogue record for this book is available from the British Library.

ISBN: 978–1–84474–523–4

Set in Dante 12/15pt
Typeset in Great Britain by CRB Associates, Potterhanworth, Lincolnshire
Printed and bound in Great Britain by Ashford Colour Press Ltd, Gosport,
Hampshire

*Inter-Varsity Press publishes Christian books that are true to the Bible and that
communicate the gospel, develop discipleship and strengthen the church for its
mission in the world.*

*Inter-Varsity Press is closely linked with the Universities and Colleges Christian
Fellowship, a student movement connecting Christian Unions in universities and
colleges throughout Great Britain, and a member movement of the International
Fellowship of Evangelical Students. Website: www.uccf.org.uk.*

For my dad
who has always shared his wisdom with me
so generously and graciously

Grateful thanks to . . .

Kate Byrom, my editor, for spotting that the research project could in fact be a book, and gently steering me through the process.

All the staff and volunteers at the Scripture Union X:site events, and Holy Trinity Church, Aylesbury, for accommodating the disruption of the research process that provided so much useful data.

My friends and family, who have been so supportive and encouraging. If you spot yourself in these pages, please take it as an indication of how much you mean to me!

All the boys who have been a source of inspiration and bewilderment, joy and amazement, boundless energy and love – especially my own son, Gideon. May God bless you and keep you, and may his face shine upon you.

CONTENTS

Preface   11

Part One
A spiritual spectrum?   17
Ways of listening   30

Part Two: Ten spiritual connections
1. Our Father
    Relationship   43
2. Muscles and mayhem
    Play   56
3. Once upon a time
    Story   69
4. Make it go away
    Pain and loss   83
5. Poo, bum, willy
    Humour   93
6. Rock and paper and scissors
    Music and creativity   99
7. Pauses and ponderings
    Thinking   108
8. The eleventh commandment
    Service   121

9. Thrills and spills
   Risk 131
10. I game, therefore I am
    Technology 142

Part Three
Go and do likewise 159

Appendix 1: Statistics on boys' childhood
experiences 163
Appendix 2: The creation of the spiritual
connections list 164
Appendix 3: The research project 167
Appendix 4: Michael Anthony's Four
Perspectives of Children's Ministry 176

Notes 181

PREFACE

This book comes with a caveat! It is about boys, and shares a passion about boys and developing their spirituality within a Christian faith framework. It is not, however, a magic potion and I am well aware that, as a woman in her forties, there are many things about being a boy that I do not know! Nonetheless, I grew up with a brother, I have one son and two godsons, and I have worked with boys for over twenty-five years. Please forgive the generalizations, and instead use the discussions and ideas as a starting point for developing your own understanding of boys, and join the debate that raises awareness of the beauty, wonder and fragility of children's spirituality. I am a Christian, and this work has a faith-based frame of reference and reflects my belief that spirituality is a God-given attribute, as we are made in God's image. I am hoping, however, that it will not only be informed by non-faith-based understandings of spirituality, but also contribute to the general discussions on this subject and be useful to those working with boys in schools and other secular organizations.

'I am so glad you are doing this research: we have such a problem with our boys!' has felt like a common refrain as I have broached the subject of this study. The probability is that boys are not actually the problem, but it is our attitude that is at fault, and our ideas of what a boy really is and what he needs in order to exercise his spirituality and connect with God. Over the last few years, boys have been perceived as underachieving at school, becoming a problem in our society, and disengaging from our churches. It is my belief that part of the reason for this is that we are not meeting their spiritual needs.

In the light of the current interest in spirituality and the apparent drop in numbers of children attending church, I decided to investigate the spiritual expressions and preferences of children between the ages of five and eleven, using three different settings within the UK:

- an Anglican children's church;
- ecumenical bimonthly worship activities run by Scripture Union, called X:site;
- RE (religious education) lessons in a school.

My research findings form the foundation of this book. My hope is that they will provide some pointers on how we can all better help boys express and engage with their spirituality.

By writing about boys, I am not suggesting that boys and girls are completely different, but rather that there might be differences that need exploring more fully in order for us to give every child as many opportunities as possible to explore his or her spirituality. The purpose of this book is not to judge children for the gender role messages that they have been given and for which they are not responsible, or to make unwarranted suppositions about their natures. Instead, the purpose is to ask, 'So what do we do now?' about what we find to be true about the boys and girls with whom we work, and then to ask, 'How do we engage with them and enhance their engagement with God?'

The emphasis is on boys and their spirituality, but I believe that both boys and girls will engage with God, and express how they connect with him, in a range of different ways, and so there is every chance that the material in this book will be helpful for working with girls as well. Equally, although the research findings are from children in Key Stages 1 and 2 of primary education (five- to eleven-year-olds), many of the ideas are appropriate for pre-schoolers. There is evidence to suggest that the pattern of religious or spiritual experiences, and children's ability to make sense of them, changes as they grow up; so again, although some of the suggestions may be applicable to teenage boys, it is as well to be aware of the variances caused by adolescence and the transition to secondary school.

Each chapter includes a 'So how . . . ' section, with ideas on how you can put some of the thinking into practice, and concludes with some questions for you, your children's work team (if you have one) and your church leaders to think about. Where I have used the ideas or research findings of other writers, they are referenced in the notes at the end of the book, so that if something catches your interest you know where to go to find out about it in more detail. The chapter entitled 'Ways of listening' gives a brief overview of how I did the research – not solely to validate the findings, but rather to suggest ways in which you too can 'listen' to the boys you are working with to find out what is true for them.

PART ONE
A SPIRITUAL SPECTRUM

A SPIRITUAL SPECTRUM?

Sometimes it only takes a word to release our innermost concerns. In the case of this mother it was the word 'characters'. Used to describe, amongst others, her nine-year-old son, it had opened the floodgates. Sobbing, she expressed her fears and worries about the negative attention he had been getting at school. I stood bemused. As his children's church leader I had only ever known him as a kind, loving, energetic and life-filled boy and, as I tried to reassure her, 'one of the most spiritual children I know'.

Being spiritual does not make us an A-grade student, Mother Teresa or a professor of theology. Neither does it make us a hippy or a geek. The way we experience God is as varied as our personalities, and, of course, subject to our relationship with the Spirit. 'Spirituality' has become a bit of a buzzword in some circles, but many of us still struggle to know what it really means, and some of us even struggle to believe that it really exists, or that it is significant in children's development and well-being. Despite data to suggest that children do have a variety of spiritual experiences, this is still not recognized in any textbooks on child development or psychology.[1] And so there is an interesting gap between theory and practice. In the UK, the Office for Standards in Education (Ofsted) is required to assess whether schools are offering their pupils opportunities to develop their spirituality and yet most teachers will not have been taught much, if anything, about spirituality and what is required to encourage it.

This lack of understanding is not just in educational circles. Many Christians still struggle with the concept of spirituality, concerned that if we describe spirituality as a human capacity and talk of spirit without a capital 'S', it muddies the water and detracts from the omnipotence of God and the salvation of Jesus. Let me be clear that although I believe that all children are spiritual beings, capable of engaging with and expressing that spirituality, I also believe that not all expressions of spirituality are healthy. We are designed to be in relationship with God, through Jesus, so the ultimate expression of our spirituality is in that relationship. But the breath of God that Genesis describes as moving over the waters and forming the very foundations of life on this planet is still foundational, and just as the Celtic Christians believed that there were 'thin' places where heaven and earth touched, I believe that we have 'thin' places in our hearts and minds where we can 'connect' with that breath, whether we can name it or not; and for children those places are 'thinner' and more accessible.

This can put our children in danger as their openness and naivety make them vulnerable to unhealthy as well as healthy spiritual expressions. We must, however, be careful that our genuine desire to protect them does not stifle and limit them either. Perhaps the key test we can apply as we ponder ways in which to encourage boys in particular to grow in their spirituality is whether that 'connection' is facing in the direction of God or away from him.

So what is spirituality?

There have been times when studying this topic has felt a bit like picking up runny jelly with your hands. Either it runs between your fingers or, when you feel you have a substantial enough 'pile', it just flops over, sliding back onto the plate. Gordon Mursell reminds us that the word 'spirit' originates from the Latin term *spiritus*, the primary meaning of which is 'breath' – something physical and yet invisible. This word also has an important secondary meaning: 'inspiration', which literally means 'breathing in' and implies those physical but invisible qualities like love, courage, peace and truth. This understanding is also reflected in the Hebrew word *ruach*, which means both 'breath' and 'spirit' and is used quite often when talking about the action of God.[2]

Although the Hebrew theological tradition sought to hold the physical and spiritual together, it is believed that much Christian thought has been influenced by the work of Plato, who deemed what is good 'spiritual' (invisible, incorporeal, immortal) and what is bad 'physical'. Hence 'spirituality' is considered by many as a 'world-denying discipline' or at least a redirection of physical drives and longings to the life of the spirit. Perhaps this is why some have considered children incapable of experiencing, expressing and understanding spirituality, or at the very best being limited in their ability to do so. However, Kathryn Copsey, in her wonderful book about children's spirituality called *From the Ground Up*, argues that this is exactly why children's spirituality is important – because they do not make the distinction between the sacred and the secular, the holy and the profane.[3]

Thanks to the research of people like David Hay and Rebecca Nye,[4] it is now widely believed that spiritual awareness is an ordinary aspect of children's experience. In fact, it is a key part of children's developmental journey as they strive to understand not only what is happening to them, but also why.

Some have given spirituality a straightforward definition like 'an awareness that there is something Other, something greater than the course of everyday events'.[5] Others, such as Hay and Nye, believe that it is more complex than that. Amongst the definitions I have explored, it would appear that the strongest theme is concerned with how we sense we are connected to ourselves, others, the world / universe and the transcendent. Spiritual relations are not just about the individual and God. While many of the definitions or descriptions of spirituality do refer to this relational aspect and the ensuing sense of community, many also talk about an 'interior life' and the search for meaning and purpose and answers to questions like 'Who am I? Where do I fit in? Why am I here?'

Spirituality is a multifaceted dimension of the human experience and therefore we cannot be too prescriptive or simplistic in our definitions, but I wonder if this is in fact what the Western church has done. The denominational differences, which serve us in part, also do us a disservice as they reinforce the 'little boxes' in which we relate to God. I teach the 'Worship and Spirituality' module at Oxford CYM,[6] and part of the remit of this module is to open up the eyes of the students to different forms of Christian spirituality and the possibilities they might bring to their work with children and young people. One of my proudest moments was when one of the students, with tears in his eyes, spoke about how the module – which included a retreat in a Roman Catholic monastery,

'Godly Play' (which I explore in chapter 2, 'Muscles and mayhem') and an outdoor Celtic service – had changed his life, opening up ways of connecting with God that he had previously dismissed as old-fashioned and irrelevant. If this passionate youth worker and spiritual leader felt he had previously been missing out, then just what is happening to all the other boys and men? How are their natural preferences for expressing their spirituality being served by their church, their school and their local community?

Spirituality and physicality

Nevertheless, to define spirituality purely in terms of the ethereal and experiential is to do it an injustice. I love liberation theologian Gustavo Gutiérrez's argument that spirituality is about 'taking over the historical practice of Jesus', which means making the world of the poor our own as we live out our relationship with God together.[7] Giving children space and attention to grow and develop, to dwell and observe with clarity, will not only reap dividends in the form of increased strength of character, but will also have an impact on their relationship with other people, their community, those in need and the world which we have been given to steward.

As I read and reread many definitions and descriptions of children's spirituality, and spirituality in general, I began to wonder if the emphasis was too much on thoughts and feelings (the cognitive and affective domains). Of course these are both important, but what about those (perhaps often boys) who live more in the physical domain? Is this concentration on the ethereal and the internal limiting their ability to engage with and express their spirituality? In the same way that the writer of *Multiple Intelligences*, Howard Gardner,[8] argued that intelligence does not exist in one domain or faculty, I would argue that neither does spirituality, and that there are a whole spectrum of activities, experiences and encounters that enable us to make connections and relationships, feel awe and wonder, identify meaning and purpose, and get a sense of 'other', as well as connect with God.

Endangered dragonflies?

Boys' spirituality can be likened to a dragonfly. While seemingly delicate and frail, the dragonfly is a creature of immense strength and stamina. At a distance it can seem like an ethereal jewel; up close it has muscularity and speed, and even a slightly frightening aspect with those big eyes like limitless pools. Incredible and beautiful, the dragonfly is under constant threat from predators and the destruction of its natural habitat. Also incredible and beautiful, boys' spirituality is under similar threat from a society that measures success and value in pounds and column inches, and from a church that seems for many boys and young men to be irrelevant and boring.

In the last ten years more and more people have taken seriously the notion that children do have an 'innate spirituality',[9] and have started to question whether this is being harmed or limited by the culture in which we live.[10] Although religion is an expression of spirituality and not necessarily its source, it is worrying that according to Church of England reports, the number of children attending Sunday school (an indication of some level of faith, or at least family attendance at church) is dropping by an average of 2.5% per year. Similar drops in attendance are being experienced by most of the large denominations in the UK.[11] But while it appears that church attendance is a sign that people in general are becoming less religious, it would be a mistake to assume therefore that they are becoming less spiritual.

Although some may believe that spirituality is on the increase, others have expressed concerns about what has been described as the spiritual vacuum experienced by many men and boys. Often in the minority in church congregations, holiday clubs or associated children's groups, are they getting what they need to help them connect with God in ways that are meaningful and appropriate to them? In a culture that separates boys from girls at birth with pink or blue buggies and gender-specific toys, is the church offering boys a spirituality that is boy-shaped, and if not, does it need to?

Well, the answer is complex. The information I collected certainly seems to indicate that preferences for engaging and expressing spirituality do not always have a significant gender bias; lots of ways to connect with God are enjoyed by both boys and girls, men and women. However, my perception is that in church we tend to limit the range of ways in which children (and adults) are encouraged to connect with God. And the ways that *are* offered tend to be those that are preferred by women and girls.

For instance, in church, worship might entail large amounts of reading aloud, or singing 'Jesus is my boyfriend' songs (emotive lyrics with ballad-style accompaniment), followed perhaps by coffee and a chat. In children's church, meanwhile, reading very small text to a group, sitting still or dancing with complicated actions might be the kinds of behaviour that are expected.

There are writers who suggest that young men and women inhabit and shape quite different world-views which include strikingly different approaches to things like motivation and behaviour, even in pre-schoolers. Research has indeed found differences between male and female emotional responses, and religious experiences among adults.[12] There is also a great deal of statistical evidence (see appendix 1) to suggest that boys and girls are getting a different experience of childhood. There is, however, the academic camp which argues that there is not the gender division we try to make with pink or camouflage lunchboxes, action toys or Barbie!

This book sits with a foot in both camps. There are children who exhibit behaviour and characteristics at extreme ends of the masculine-to-feminine spectrum, but there are also an awful lot who mill around in the middle. Many of us know children who do not fit the stereotypes. One of my son's best friends is a girl: they play the same games, climb trees, cycle round the block together and sit side by side in an armchair to watch the same programmes. She is physically courageous and jumps from heights that he struggles to reach. He is gregarious and loving and has often been her spokesperson.

It is my belief that in the same way that children have different preferences for ways of playing and learning, they also have different ways of engaging with and expressing their spirituality. The problem with highlighting gender is that it may lead to a labelling of children that is not necessarily helpful and, rather than helping them to realize their potential as individuals, encourages them to conform to particular stereotypes. But the reality is that if we have a group of children which includes those with specific needs, and we treat them all exactly the same, then that will lead to inequalities being left unaddressed. In the same way, if boys do have slightly different propensities and preferences in how they express and experience their spirituality and connect with God, we need to make sure that these are offered and enhanced.

Spiritual connections

I have explored a range of activities that relate to children's spirituality and encompass the children's physical reality as well as their thoughts and feelings. (Appendix 2 describes how this list of 'spiritual connections' started to emerge and be drawn together.) As I played with the list of 'connections', it became clear that they could be described as falling under five broad categories.

1. Relational (connecting with others)
2. Aesthetic (using beauty as a connection)
3. Active (engaging through the body)
4. Intrapersonal (connecting on my own)
5. Ritualistic (connecting through ritual)

However, many of them either overlap with each other or could, quite comfortably, sit in another category. The purpose of this book is to look at what boys have said about this list and to get *us* thinking about how it is reflected in the spirituality of those with whom we work or live.

For instance, one of the key discoveries for me was that I had underestimated how much *feelings* would be a part of each and every connection, not just the ones that have an obvious link. They are not a connection on their own, but rather have a web-like presence throughout the list. And again, it was also only as I worked through the data that the importance of *technology* in the spiritual lives of children, particularly boys, emerged.

For the sake of simplicity I have bunched up some of the connections to create chapters that explore bigger themes related to a cluster of findings. The ten spiritual connections are as follows.

1. Relationship
2. Play
3. Story

4. Pain and loss
5. Humour
6. Music and creativity
7. Thinking
8. Service
9. Risk
10. Technology

What saddens me is that many of these ways of engaging with God are, at best, not encouraged and, at worst, discouraged by the church and various Christian children's activities. Recently we had a new team member join us at a holiday club. One of the things that struck her about what we did, she said, was the quiet and the order. Yes, we did have moments of madness and mayhem, noise and chaos, but her experience of children's ministry was that this was all there was, that the children were not given the opportunity also to experience stillness and quiet, order and calm, space and ritual. My hope from the research project and this subsequent book is that identifying some of the range of spiritual connections that children use can help us not to restrict expression and experience, but rather to offer a wider range of opportunities to all the children with whom we share our lives.

There is still little research specifically into the impact of gender on children's spirituality. As I tested whether the list of spiritual connections is in fact a genuine representation of what is going on for children, I also sought to discover whether there was a gender bias to the connections that they used. In general I still believe that, just like Gardner's Intelligences mentioned above, children will instinctively lean towards a number of connections both because of their nature and because of the environment in which they have been nurtured. With the exception of one or two connections, the evidence from the research project did not indicate any significant gender bias. What I have done, however, is to pull out what, in particular, the boys have said or shown, to help us to think about how we can better meet their needs.

God goggles

Listening to Mark Yaconelli, the writer of *Contemplative Youth Ministry*, speaking recently, I was reminded that what I take for granted in terms of the ways I look at and experience the world is not perhaps what is going on for everyone. Most people (including many Christians) are living life as if they are watching a 3-D movie without the special glasses: they are not tuned into the sacred moments, the presence of the spiritual and the Spirit, not getting the depth of their connectivity and meaning.

It is my belief that children are born 'wearing the special glasses'. They see the world as God intended, but very quickly those glasses are taken away from them and trodden into the ground.

The ten spiritual connections are not really rocket science; they are, however, a start. What I am asking us to do is to put on our 'God goggles' and supply the children we know with a pair too. I am not saying that I have got it sorted yet by any means, but God's grace, my parents' wisdom, my own personality and experiences have enabled me to sharpen the focus of my spirituality and become more comfortable in my 'God goggles'.

Our job, as people who journey alongside children, is to practise wearing our 3-D glasses until we do not even notice them, and to encourage our children to do the same. Sometimes this will only be a case of giving the pair a child is already wearing a perfunctory wipe; for others we may have to help find them and mend them with sticky tape, and perhaps even help a child hold them on for a while. So, many of the activities described in this book as ways to enhance and develop boys' spirituality can be found in publications like *The Boy Scout Handbook*, or *A Million and One Things to Fill the School Holidays*, but the intention of this book is to look at these activities while wearing 'God goggles' and see beyond the activities to the ways in which God can use our knowledge of the children to tap into the sacred and raise their awareness of themselves, those around them, the world they live in and their supernatural God.

I believe spirituality is an ordained part of a child's being and, left to their own devices, they will use all the religious and spiritual resources available to them. The problem is that, even in our postmodern Western culture, this spirituality is at best relatively hidden and at worst actively discouraged. Celebrity culture and materialism seem to be sucking the very lifeblood from the natural spirituality of the human species and encouraging us to live at a level that is only interested in what we see on screen or in a magazine, or in what we own. I agree with the suggestion that children's spirituality is damaged from birth,[13] not just by bad or inadequate parenting, but by comments, practices or responsibilities that shut down their openness and repress their curiosity and ability to see wonder. For many of our children, those 3-D glasses or 'God goggles' really have been trampled in the dirt!

Things to think about

- What words spring to mind when you think of boys?
- Do you think boys and girls are different? If so, why?
- Are boys in your church/club/school viewed as a problem or a joy? Why?

- What is your gut feeling about the ten spiritual connections listed above?
- Which would you say are your personal preferences?
- Which do you *not* give the opportunity for your boys to use?
- How often do you wear your 'God goggles'? Do you know any boys who have had theirs smeared or even smashed? Are you ready to do something about that?

WAYS OF LISTENING

When the voices of children are heard on the green,
And laughing is heard on the hill,
My heart is at rest within my breast,
And everything else is still.[1]

I cannot stress enough how important it is to know the children with whom you are working, and that can only happen by spending time with them, listening to what they are saying (and what they are not saying), and observing how they interact with each other and the activities you provide.

I spent time listening to groups of children with whom I worked in church, in schools and at the X:site events. I was keen to see what impact a better understanding of spirituality could have on the work that I do. (Details of some of my methodology and findings can be found in appendix 3.)

Despite the fact that the emphasis of my research was the spirituality of boys in particular, I carried out this listening in mixed-gender groups, not only to test whether spiritual connections may have a gender bias, but also to avoid 'over-gendering' and the creation of findings which suggest falsely that some spiritual connections are only of interest to boys. This does not necessarily mean that your 'listening' has to be done in mixed-gender groups. Indeed, sometimes boys feel more confident in expressing their thoughts and feelings when they are just with other boys.

 So how . . . can we help boys to engage with and express their spirituality by listening to them?

Two ears, two eyes, one mouth

If we are working in a Christian or educational setting, or even just trying to bring up our own children, sometimes we are so concerned with imparting our knowledge and understanding that we forget that for a child to feel valued there is nothing that beats good old-fashioned listening. The kind that requires intermittent eye contact, body attention (by this I mean that even if you are, for instance, standing at the sink or whiteboard, some of your body, for some of the time, is turned towards the speaker) and appropriate responses and questions. It is probably helpful to have a stock of questions that can start that listening process, but remember not to make them questions that might have a 'wrong' or a 'right' answer, and be ready to shut up once the talking has begun!

It is also important that you choose the right kind of language in your questioning. This is not only to ensure that the best level of information is elicited from the children, but also because using the wrong language, particularly if it introduces a fear or mistrust of God, can be spiritually restricting. When I was discussing spirituality with children in RE lessons, for example, it was important that I shared the reality and excitement of living with a Christian faith, but equally important that I did not proselytize by declaring Jesus as the only truth and thus jeopardize the relationship that I have with the school. In the church and X:site settings, it was vital that I did not 'shut down' the children's experiences and expressions with vocabulary that they did not understand or relate to. We need to be aware of how our words can be misinterpreted, particularly those related to our style of doing church. For instance, we might feel comfortable about describing our redemption as 'being washed in the blood', but a concrete-thinking seven-year-old boy might find that the grossest thought ever! Equally we need to understand the language that the children are using. For instance, in a previous research project about using images of Jesus with children, one boy wrote that Jesus looked 'sad'. In this particular instance he did not mean melancholy: instead he thought that Jesus looked cool (not cold, but wicked; not evil, but . . . you see where I'm going with this!). We need to know what the children are actually saying, not so that we can correct their grammar, but so that we can hear them properly.

We also have two eyes and need to use them to 'hear' what the children are saying. What are the boys saying with the angle of their shoulders, the tilt of their head and the placement of their feet about how meaningful activities are and whether they are helping them to connect with God? Inactivity and/or frenetic activity does not necessarily mean that a boy is not engaging with God through this connection – we can only know by watching and learning from the clues they give us. Intriguingly, one X:site event team said that simply facilitating the research had 'opened their eyes' to the issues of boys' spirituality. They had become more aware of the use of male role models, and of the assumptions they had been making about how boys should conform to activities planned predominantly by females.

Pictures and Post-its

Many of you will already have stockpiled 'useful' pictures and 'interesting' sticky Post-it notes. Pictures are a really good way of helping boys engage with their spirituality and, perhaps not surprisingly, they do not like writing things down. So you could lay a whole load of pictures on the floor, or stick them to a wall, and ask the children to stick on different types of Post-its in response to statements like 'This makes me feel . . . ', 'This picture reminds me of . . . ', or 'These colours make me . . . ' Very soon you will find they have a great deal to tell you!

At home, a pile of postcards or photos can serve the same purpose. Sorted through one by one, or laid out on the table, they help initiate conversations that enable your boys to vocalize some of their meaning-making processes, or tell you a bit about the mechanics of their relationship with God.

'I feel . . . ' posters

I used 'I feel . . . ' posters in my research (there are further details about these in appendix 3). They were designed to encourage the children to think about more general spiritual experiences, and were large sheets of mostly blank card with the following words printed in the centre:

- 'I feel I matter when . . . '
- 'I feel I belong when . . . '
- 'I feel closest to God when . . . '

The children could then complete the statement on a Post-it note and stick this to the poster. They were allowed to complete as many or as few as they wished. You could try this too.

This was a relatively simple process but produced some very interesting results. It encouraged the boys to express their feelings, without necessarily having to talk about them. If you are doing the activity with a mixed-gender group, then you can get a better idea of what your boys are thinking and feeling by denoting gender with different-coloured Post-it notes.

Questionnaires and focus groups

Schools are catching on to the fact that 'listened-to children' tend to be more motivated, so make it clear that your listening is intentional by asking the children to complete a short and easy questionnaire or join in a focus group. Be aware of the power relations that might be present, not just in the way that the children might want to 'please' you by answering 'Jesus' to just about every question,[2] but also in the way that some children can inhibit the free expression of others.

We had some issues with 'bored boys' in our children's church, so I designed a questionnaire which asked the children to show their preferences for activities under four main headings ('being at children's church', 'worshipping God', 'engaging with the Bible' and 'praying'). Each section had a number of pictures with a title (for instance, 'playing with my friends', 'singing loud songs', 'working out what the Bible means with a quiz', 'praying quietly on my own') and the children were asked to circle all the activities they liked. Many of the choices represented different elements of Gardner's theory of Multiple Intelligences,[3] so might appeal to active learners, or interpersonal learners, or children who learn through puzzling. At the end they were asked to complete some 'I feel . . .' phrases. Their answers to the questionnaires were analysed, and this data was then used to inform leaders about what kinds of activities might work best. It also helped to form smaller groups of children who had similar preferences as well as ages. After the implementation of the changes it was generally agreed that the new format was working, and that those boys who had struggled before were now staying more focused and had contributed a great deal more to the planned activities. It could be argued that the 'settling' of the boys was because they felt that in general their needs were now being better met. This may well be true, but these perceived 'improvements' may have been because the children had felt 'heard', and that what was put in place actually freed them to engage with their spirituality in ways they could not achieve before.

Questionnaires do not have to be individual paper-based activities. How about creating a 'wall chart' (a set of large pictures and/or words with blank spaces for the children to fill in), and giving the children stickers with which to indicate their preferences? In order to elicit information from those attending X:site events, without disrupting their busy evening, we used two wall charts – one on which we asked them to indicate the ways in which they prefer to 'hear from God', and the other on which we asked them to indicate the ways in which they prefer to 'respond to God'. Each child was given three stickers ('1', '2', '3') so that they could rate their favourites. The stickers were colour-coded: red and purple for girls; green and orange for boys. The idea was that a mix of colours meant that a child was less likely to be put off placing their sticker on a preference by the dominance of one colour that indicated a different gender.

Another way to get as much information as possible in a short amount of time is to video a group discussion or focus group. Make sure that you get the parents' permission beforehand and, while keeping it low key, let the children know what is happening. It is probably better to keep the numbers in the group low so that you can keep track of what is being said by whom. Be aware that this approach may not work for all of your children, and give them opportunities to opt out if they wish. One of my videos shows an aborted discussion where two six-year-old boys refused to sit anywhere where the video camera could see them (which was fine) and did not really want to discuss their views. They each had opposing favourite activities and in the end we gave up and went and did something else. Although they did not contribute directly to the statistics, their reaction to the questioning was an important insight into how some boys might feel about this kind of discussion group!

For each group, I laid out on a long table a set of A4 sheets which depicted with words and pictures different ways to 'hear from God' and to 'respond to God'. These are set out in the table on the next page.

I then asked the children to tell me which were their favourite ways to respond to God, and which were their least favourite. Watching the videos, I realized what a fantastic opportunity this was for affirming the children's views. As I was not sure of the sound quality of the recording, when each child gave me their answer, I repeated it, nodding and affirming their choice, not because they had chosen the right answer, but because they had chosen something for themselves. As far as possible, I tried to keep my hands off the table, so that I did

Ways to hear from God	Ways to respond to God
Singing and music	With music and singing
Reading the Bible on my own or with others	By helping people
Learning Bible verses in fun ways and thinking about them later	By looking after God's creation
Talking about God and Jesus with others	With dancing and jumping about
Working out what things mean with quizzes and puzzles	By trusting God when doing something a bit scary
Acting out Bible stories	By making things and being creative
Listening to someone telling a Bible story or praying	Praying quietly on my own
Looking at pictures or at God's creation	Praying in a small group
Feeling God's presence when I am nervous or excited	Doing something that represents my prayers
When I am doing something that represents my prayers	By writing something
Watching Bible stories being acted out or as films or cartoons	By thinking and making plans
Thinking and wondering about God and the Bible on my own	Looking at things and thinking 'Wow'

not inadvertently indicate which sheets they 'should' be choosing. This meant that (to the great amusement of my own children) there was a great deal of nodding and eyebrow affirmation going on!

One interesting activity to do as part of this process is to ask the group to indicate some kind of 'order of importance' for whatever it is that they have been discussing. This is an excellent opportunity to observe how much the boys are being influenced by each other and/or the girls in the group, and how much they are prepared to stick to their own preferences.

Thumbs up, thumbs down

Some writers[4] express concern that research carried out in schools is done with 'captive subjects', where the balance of power is in the hands of the adults and not the children. The same could be true of church activities or after-school clubs where the children are taken or left by their parents. Although the children may not have much choice about attending your activity, it is important that they are given some choices. In the RE lessons we developed a system whereby at the end of each session the children were able to have a say about what went on. Every child was given a double-sided card with which to respond to a number of statements made; one side had a smiling face and thumbs up, the other side had a frowning face and thumbs down. The statements included classroom methodologies as well as aspects of spirituality with which the children could express agreement or disagreement. If they did not want to, or could not decide, then they were asked to hold their card horizontally, thereby giving them the choice of opting out.

Friendly feedback

One of the advantages of having a scribe in the RE lessons was that she too heard everything that went on, and we were able to 'debrief' after each session was over. This meant that we could look at events or comments from two different angles, and fill in the gaps as to possible causes and results. Sometimes at the end of a long day or session we all just want to put our feet up or go home, but it is important to try to take some time – sooner rather than later – to talk with the people who have been helping you look after your boys about what you have heard and seen. Your observations might help someone else work better with a particular child; theirs might help you understand why another child just does not engage in the way you had hoped.

Photo opportunity

It would appear from the research data that not only do many boys find visual images a good source of stimulation for connecting and engaging, but they also struggle to verbalize a spirituality or faith that is perhaps deeply held but not lightly shared. One approach is to use digital camera technology to help them think about and express how they connect with God and their spirituality. Perhaps they could explore their responses to the three 'I feel . . . ' statements given above by taking photos that show or represent where they feel they matter, belong and/or are closest to God. Or they could produce a video diary, or take pictures of their 'thin places' where they experience awe and wonder, or are able to ponder deeply and make meanings. Depending on the nature of your work with them, you can have it as a programmed activity or ask them to do it for a week at home and bring in the results.

You could even do it as a family, perhaps building up a scrapbook that represents different elements of the year.

Things to think about

- What jargon do you use as part of your communication about your faith that might be hard for children (particularly those who are unchurched) to interpret?
- What are the 'in' words amongst the boys with whom you are working? What do they actually mean?
- In what ways can you find out more about the boys in your group/community?
- How can you be a more effective advocate for listening to children, and in particular boys?

PART TWO
TEN SPIRITUAL CONNECTIONS

1. OUR FATHER
RELATIONSHIP

The blond hair popped up over the flimsy fence again, and the mouth that soon followed was in full flow. 'My dad has . . . and then my dad . . . and did you know my dad can . . . ' The parents of this gorgeous four-year-old boy stood inside their caravan wincing, as once again he stood on a chair and regaled the bemused holiday-makers next door with interesting facts about his father and the amazing feats he was capable of performing . . .

It has been said that, left to their own devices, children will create an image of God based on their perception of their parents.[1] This little boy will have no problem in believing that God is a God of love and that Jesus can do amazing things. Fathers are really important for all children, especially boys, as they shape their masculine identity with reference to what they see and learn from them.[2] I really do not wish to hurt or alienate those whose relationship with their own father is painful, or those whose children do not have a 'live-in' father, but God's best plan for the family is a mother *and* a father, and then children. There are all sorts of reasons why this does not happen, and rather than float in cloud cuckoo land, the purpose of this chapter is to deal with what is rather than what could be. For this reason, it looks at the importance of relationships with men and women, within the family (our biological fathers and mothers) and in our church activities (our spiritual fathers and mothers), and the impact that these have on boys' spirituality.

Secure foundations

Freud's belief that the format, condition and quality of children's relationships with people of their own or the opposite sex are laid down in the first six years of life has been corroborated by several empirical studies and so, for most children, the relationships they have with their parents are key to their understanding of love and trust. Identity formation is also closely linked with relationship and much has been written about how our idea of 'self' develops through our relationships with other people. If you are lucky enough to hold a new baby when he is awake, his eyes constantly search your face and his mouth forms shapes in response to yours. We connect with others from the moment we are born.

Key writers on faith development[3] cite love from a parent as a foundational step in that development, and it is not difficult to see how parents not only help form our 'unconscious theology' and inform our impression of God, but are also instrumental in promoting or inhibiting spiritual formation and transformation. Several of the children mentioned their parents in their 'I feel . . . ' statements, and it was interesting that when asked to indicate whether they had a faith or not, many of the children in the RE lessons made reference to family members. It seems to me, then, that it is vitally important that we seek to encourage families, and in particular parents, in their fostering of spirituality and faith development.

There is a great deal of evidence to show just how important fathers are in the development of emotionally healthy children,[4] but in his research Stephen Frosh also identified that most of the boys he spoke to felt that this relationship was ineffective.[5] I wonder how many of the fathers of the boys we are working with actually feel equipped and supported to care for their children in a way that enhances their spirituality and does not damage it. Changing this may require some radical rethinking in our church life, or just some simple changes in the way we communicate or do things.

I was very privileged to grow up with a father in ministry, who was often around when I got home from school. At this point in the day we did not talk much, we did not do much, in fact we mainly used to sit and watch *Dogtanian and the Three Muskehounds* together, but he was there for me for that time. As my own children came along, I was aware that due to work and travel pressures my husband was unable to enjoy this time with his children. I had to consciously make that time for them in the day and then, when he came home, walk away from whatever bedtime task was in hand so that he could complete it. Things might not have been done in the style or timescale that I would have preferred, but it was so important that he had some precious time on his own with his children.

Parenting as a team sport

Dave Andrews, in his thinking about community, talks about the Trinity as a model for community development,[6] suggesting that where there are two in relationship there is a line of communication, but where three are in relationship, the triangular lines of communication create not only stability but also space. He believes that God intentionally models this triune relationship to encourage us to create those spaces that are an invitation for others to dwell in and enjoy the presence of God. Using this model for a family context may start to get a bit tricky: a trinitarian relationship between two parents and a child might be God's best plan, but in no way does he judge those for whom that is not the case, and let's not get so hooked up on numbers that we forget that the national average for the number of children in a family is two and a half! The key principles are helpful, however: triangles are more stable and more spacious than lines, and there needs to be space and balance in these relationships.

Parenting is a team sport! What can the church do to 'scaffold' where one parent is providing the majority of the childcare, for whatever reason? Without judging or patronizing, but instead providing some of the space and balance that a triune community-based relationship offers. When one of my best friends died suddenly, her husband was left on his own with three children and a baby. One of the dear old ladies from our church visited regularly and looked after the children while he went out for a walk or a run. She loved being with those children, they loved having her around, and he loved the space that she provided.

Statistically speaking, single parents are more likely to be women, which means that many children are growing up in households where men play either no part, or only a temporary part. Certainly on one of the social housing estates I work on, the society is predominantly matriarchal. It is therefore really important, when we run a holiday club there, that there are as many men as possible, old and young, as part of the team, giving both boys and girls the opportunities to relate to men in a healthy and love-filled way. It is important that we think creatively about what male role models we are giving boys, not just in terms of the lack of them, but also in terms of the functions they take on within the programme of activities.

Relational connections

If so much of spirituality and indeed faith development is about relationship, does this make it difficult for men and boys who are sometimes described as less emotionally literate? There is a general perception, with some corroborating evidence, that females have more accomplished verbal skills and are better at empathizing; and that males have better spacial awareness and are more able to 'systemize' data.[7] There are also statistics that show that you are four times more likely to have autism or Asperger's (syndromes that have an impact on your ability to relate to others) if you are male.[8] If this is the case, then does this imply that for some boys and young men the 'relational' side of spirituality and faith may be more difficult to connect with? Well yes, if we only count relationship in terms of conversation, in its narrowest sense. Not many of us hear the voice of God out loud on a daily basis, or have conversations with him in quite the same way as Moses did, but we do know that we have a relationship with him – a relationship based on 'presence' and using other forms of communication as additional sources of knowledge and growth.

Our relationships with boys require expression through conversation, touch and service. It is my concern that in this world of 'child protection' where, quite rightly, we are doing our utmost to protect children and the people who work with them, we are also in danger of damaging those important relationships by discouraging the appropriate touching that is such a necessary part of that relationship. For children who experience life vividly through their senses, touch can be an important element of that sensual spiritual connection. My experience in working with boys aged from nought to fourteen years has shown just how important physical contact – 'rough and tumble' – is for boys who seek it out, and therefore it is covered in more detail in the next chapter, 'Muscles and mayhem'.

Let's not, however, get carried way with this idea that boys are incommunicative physical masses. Most of us have spent time with boys who never seem to draw breath in their verbal stream of consciousness. Boys *do* like to talk about things that interest them, and many of them *are* interested in religious and spiritual matters. They just need the opportunities to talk about the things that matter to them, or puzzle them, or cause them to wonder. The fact that 'talking about God and Jesus with others' as a means of hearing from God was a higher preference for the boys who attended the X:site events than for the girls indicates that this is true. It also reflects the findings of research carried out amongst boys in London aged from eleven to fourteen, which showed that when boys believe they are being listened to, they are more than willing and able to talk seriously about the things that matter to them.[9] A genuine conversation requires investment from both particip-ants without dominance or judging. Quite often in conversation children are not necessarily expecting an answer to their ponderings or questions, but simply want to be listened to and 'wondered' with.

For those boys who do find 'conversation' difficult, then perhaps other ways of verbalizing their experiences should be found. My middle daughter does a lot of her deepest expres-sion through a journal, in which she writes her hardest questions and talks about or draws her greatest fears or hurts.

She leaves it on my bed before she goes to bed, for me to read and write an answer. What I have come to realize over the years is that the answer does not always have to be profound, but sometimes just an acknowledgment that I have heard her. In the research, many of the boys indicated that they really did not like writing things down; clearly a journal may not work for them! So how do we give them the opportunity of communicating their thoughts and feelings without conversation? What about using resources like pictures and photos, or magnetic words that you can stick on a metal board, or exploring the opportunities given by technology, like SMS texts?

Spiritual parents

It is clear from the variations in responses between the different X:site events that other factors are affecting the preferences of the children, and I believe that the most important of these is the leaders. Albert Bandura (who, incidentally, has been described as one of the greatest psychologists of all time) argues that most human behaviour is learned observationally. We can tell a child to do something, or to believe something, or that something is good, but unless we are demonstrating that to be true, they will not respond. Children engage with their spirituality through narrative at events where there are good storytellers, and at other events where there is great sung worship, they will identify this as a preference. When he washed his disciples' feet, Jesus himself demonstrated that he believed that modelling is an effective method for changing a theological understanding into a behavioural reality. It is therefore of paramount importance that leaders themselves are seen to use and experiment with a number of ways to engage with and express their own spirituality, as well as encourage them in the boys. For this reason I am so proud of the young men who help as part of the Aylesbury Scripture Union Family Mission – who fetch drinks, move chairs, make fools of themselves doing the actions, have a go at the craft (and still have the energy to organize a game of football), expressing their spirituality and their faith in many different ways, some right outside their comfort zone.

Relationships are, however, much more significant than just as a vehicle for modelling. Leading thinkers in intellectual development believe that relationships are so fundamental that it is only through them that 'the self' develops.[10] In our current cultural climate where strangers are to be feared, children are making fewer connections with adults outside their families. Christian volunteers who have been police checked and validated by their agency are, therefore, in a privileged position of offering adult–child friendships that the children might not get elsewhere.

It is also important that these relationships are just that, friendships, and that the adults do not fall into the trap of believing that they are only teacher–pupil relationships. If we look back on our own childhood, I am sure that our memories of special people are of those who above all showed a trusting, loving acceptance of us, and a capacity for playfulness. If we use the metaphor of journey to think about spiritual life, we can then understand that we are travelling *alongside* the children on this path. Sometimes it might be rocky, and we might need to support the child; it may be steep and they have to drag us up the slope; we might see some funny things along the way to laugh at together; or we might have some very deep and meaningful conversations. What is essential, though, is that we are travelling together.

Writing to the Romans about the importance of the body of Christ, Paul was way ahead of contemporary psychologists who suggest that cognitive development is essentially a social process. Children grow and develop as they interact with others, and learn to feel comfortable about engaging with their spirituality as they watch others. It is therefore important that we give our boys the opportunity to interact with a small group of other children. In these smaller groups they can find the security to have those conversations they so desperately want to have, and the group facilitator can 'scaffold' their experimentation with their spirituality and faith development. The key to making this successful is facilitating – not teaching, but instead stepping back and letting the children learn from each other. Maybe it requires giving them greater creative freedom as they produce dramatic interpretations of the Bible passage, or discussing what today's theme might have to do with their life. Maybe it requires us to be silent as a conversation heads into unknown territory. I know that often time can feel a pressure, and we are so desperate for them to grow in their knowledge of Christ that we want them to 'stick to the point', but peer-led learning can allow them to meander to the point in a way that actually sticks for them!

 So how . . . do we encourage boys to engage with their spirituality through relationship and conversation?

Motivate the men!

There has to be a radical change in the attitude of the church towards ministry amongst children. It is not the poor cousin, it is the foundation of Jesus' upside-down kingdom. When the work with the children is given the status it deserves, then I suspect that more men will want to be part of it, not because they necessarily only choose roles with status, but rather because they will realize just how important it is to make a difference in the lives of boys and girls at an early age, and to offer them opportunities to grow spiritually as well as physically and mentally. If more men are involved, I believe more boys will be inspired!

The flip side of the coin is that we also need to allow men in. Recently in a church staff meeting we were discussing the arrangements for Mothering Sunday. It was agreed that the children and all the men from the congregation would go into the hall to do an activity, while all the women stayed in the church. We discussed child protection issues, and then moved on to what we would do with the crèche. The comment was made that, of course, we would have to leave that to the female team. I looked around at the four men in the staff team, two of whom were fathers and two of whom were trained youth workers. 'Aren't you insulted, that the implication is that because you're men, you're incapable of looking after babies and toddlers?' I asked. Even in a church where we are constantly striving to improve our provision for our children, we had fallen into the trap of thinking that looking after children is woman's work!

Honorary uncles

Throughout the Old Testament, other family members play an important part in the lives of the people whom God chose to make a difference in his world. In our society, where often family breakdown and employment opportunities have scattered families all over the country, our children have lost the benefit of advice, friendship and gentle discipline from the wider family. There must be many men in our churches who have either never had a longed-for child, or whose children have grown up and left home, who would love to make a difference in the lives of boys in their community who have few or no male role models around them.

I am aware that potentially we are heading into a child protection nightmare here, but let's not get deterred by the views of the world. Most men have only good intentions towards children and should be given the opportunity to express them. What we have to do as a church community or as project leaders is to 'scaffold' the situation, so that there is no opportunity for anything untoward to happen or even be perceived to happen, by making the right kinds of checks and policies, and by giving opportunities for men and boys to socialize in appropriate and safe ways.

Dads and lads

Many churches have already cottoned on to the benefits of holding 'dads and lads' events. These might take the form of gatherings around bacon sarnies, or more organized activities. Perhaps they can even include some of the ideas outlined in the chapter entitled 'Thrills and spills'! The danger of the title 'dads and lads' is that it might exclude those who cannot bring a dad. The important thing, however, is that boys are given the opportunity to be with men, so this is where 'honorary uncles' come into their own.

Practise presence

For my son, one of the most important things I can do is sit and watch television with him. He does not want me to comment on it, he is not particularly bothered what we watch (although we do have our favourites) – what he wants is my presence. And as we squash up in the armchair next to the television (the sofa is too far away for him to see and me to hear!), my presence communicates to him the depth of my care for him and just how important he is.

Sometimes, as we run busy programmes, we might struggle to find the time to make contact with each and every member of our group, and it is even harder, when we do get to have a conversation with them, if that conversation seems to be stilted and going nowhere. Youth workers have known for a long time that 'hanging out' is an important part of their work, and perhaps it is time for children's workers to pick up this idea and accept that for some of the boys, doing whatever-it-is alongside them is the best way of communicating acceptance and unconditional love.

Create conversation

The benefits of 'side-by-side' chats will be discussed in another chapter, but we also need to create opportunities for boys to discuss things in small groups, with and without girls. Once again the key is knowing your boys and who works best with whom, as well as empowering leaders and helpers to facilitate the conversation. Not to force it, but instead to nudge it in a particular direction; not to steer it, but instead to ask the right kinds of questions that connect to the thoughts and feelings the boys have. Sometimes this requires nerves of steel as the conversation meanders inevitably to bodily functions or television, and sometimes it will require the patience of a saint as you wait for someone to say something!

Intentional modelling

If you have not already done so, take a look at the list of spiritual connections (see p. 9, or the chapter headings of part 2) and try to decide which ones are your natural preferences and why. Perhaps you need to do it as a team, to find out which leaders will be able to help children explore which particular spiritual connections; or as a parent, to decide where you can develop areas for intentional modelling, showing your children that you are comfortable with expressing and engaging with your spirituality in a number of different ways, or are at least prepared to take the 'risk' of experimenting. If you want to explore your spiritual preferences further, then why not look at the material produced by Gary Thomas, called *Sacred Pathways*,[11] which relates spiritual disciplines to Myers-Briggs personality styles. Once you have a better idea of where your own preferences and prejudices are, then you will be able to identify which areas you need to work on so that you are giving your boys the broadest possible spectrum of spiritual engagement.

Things to think about

- What are your own theological understandings of gender and family roles? How might these affect the work that you do?
- Which men might God be calling to get involved in working with children?
- Encourage your church or school to deliver parenting courses like the 'Family Time' course,[12] and 'Survival Skills for Christian Parents' from Scripture Union.[13]
- Who are the key influencers to get things changed, and what conversations do you need to have with them?
- What kind of training might your team need to enhance their ability to work with small groups?

2. MUSCLES AND MAYHEM
PLAY

'Warp factor four!' The captain spoke from his high-backed leather chair. As second-in-command, she pushed buttons on the stone control panel in front of her. 'Aye, aye, captain!' she said, and off they zoomed into outer space. When they arrived (with a staged jolt) they climbed out of their spaceship and explored the planet on which they had landed. It didn't matter that to the outward eye it looked exactly the same as all the other planets they had landed on in this park up the road from their nan's house; or that out of necessity the big rocks which minutes before had been the spaceship now became potential hiding places for aliens, or storage pods for their collections of berry and leaf food. As the brother and sister played, they created what they needed through imagination, creativity and sometimes a little bit of negotiation! This was their job, this was what they did all day, or at least until they got hungry, tired or fell out over who was going to be the captain.

Four commonly accepted features of play are that:

1. it is pleasurable and enjoyable;
2. children do not play because they have to, they play because they cannot help themselves – it is spontaneous and freely chosen;
3. it involves active engagement;
4. it does not require us to be able to read or write, or even to have a particularly wide vocabulary.[1]

In churches I have often heard that the children are going out to their 'classes', or at best 'activities', but have never heard the church leader say that the children are going out to 'play'. And yet is that not what we want? Do we not desire with our whole hearts that our boys will spontaneously and freely choose an active engagement with their faith and spirituality that gives them pleasure and enjoyment? We need to take more seriously the claim that the work of the child is actually to play, and consider what implications this has on their spiritual development and the way we encourage it.

While 'play' is an important part of the underlying philosophy of Berryman's 'Godly Play'[2] approach to spirituality, and games are an integral part of curriculum material like Scripture Union's 'Light', the 'play' that is encouraged is often calm and quiet and/or specifically related to the theme. The trouble with a structured programme (a subject that we will consider later) is that it is just that – structured. While it may be slow and ritualistic, or fast-paced and attractive in its variety, it lacks the freedom that so many children crave after a week in ordered activities at school. Perhaps we need to consider offering boys more freedom to play, and opportunities to engage in lots of different types of play.

The benefits of giving children a degree of freedom to play (especially outside) are well documented,[3] but I wonder if for many children's leaders there is a fear that, if the children are not entertained with a fun-packed, theologically worthwhile programme, they are letting them down, or will be let down by their behaviour becoming out of control – neither of which is necessarily true. Joseph Chilton Pearce believes that the freedom to play is a 'divine right' and a 'foundation on which intelligence and creativity grow',[4] and I agree that in fact a brisk structure can militate against some aspects of learning and development and undermine opportunities for children to explore their creativity and dream their dreams.

Mock fighting and superheroes

Various research projects[5] have found that boys tend to be engaged in more rough-and-tumble play than girls, but interestingly our attitudes towards this have changed over the years to the extent that many educational institutions now have a zero tolerance policy for any play that involves suggestions of mock fighting or superhero combat. Penny Holland[6] critiques this zero tolerance of war and superhero games in nursery schools, and gives a great deal of anecdotal evidence of the damage inflicted by zero tolerance to boys' self-esteem and ability to enter into imaginative play. She also underlines the positive effects of a change in policy. In her research Holland discovered that once boys were allowed to use their chosen entry point into imaginative play, they were observed to extend very quickly their representational play activities and begin to flourish in many of the other pre-school activities. What implications does this have for Christian children's ministry, where mock fighting and so on is often limited due to the link with aggression, and where calm, controlled play is often encouraged?

Imaginative play has an important role to play in a child's development of strategies to cope with reality, and many also believe that it has an impact on the understanding of sacraments and liturgy.[7] If this is true, then surely limiting any element of boys' normal play could mean that we are in danger of limiting their ongoing spiritual and faith development. In *Through the Eyes of a Child*, Rebecca Nye humbly admits that had she followed her natural inclination to shut down the boys' seemingly pointless paper plane throwing at the end of a session, she would have cut off a whole avenue of spiritual exploration and experience for them.[8]

In addition, if, as some writers have suggested,[9] boys use rough play, war play and superhero play as a way of making sense of their gender, and we are in the business of offering holistic care that nurtures the body, mind and spirit of the child, then perhaps we should be prepared to give boys the opportunity to express themselves in this way more often. We need to learn the skill of watching and waiting, giving the boys time to work through whatever they are working through in their play, rather than shutting it down prematurely because it does not seem 'nice'.

There is a caveat, however. While superheroes and knights may be worthwhile playfellows in that they encourage a sense of worth and help boys to work out their place in this world, there is a very thin line between encouraging imaginative play and encouraging a revelling in gore, death and destruction that seems to be played out on so many of the 12-plus video games. It goes back to what we were talking about in terms of what spirituality is, and how not all expressions of spirituality are healthy and helpful. This is about us discerning where that line is for the boys with whom we work, and indeed helping them to learn how to discern it for themselves. Killing monsters might be OK (although Doctor Who often shows regret at having to do this) – in fact it might be helpful if a boy is wrestling with 'dark shadows' in his life, but what about when the 'enemy' becomes human? At what stage does delivering 'rough justice' to a burglar become the kind of spirituality that turns dangerous and psychotic?

Psychologists who have worked with children who have committed atrocities suggest that a diet of violence does feed the complexity of needs of a probably already severely damaged child, but there is little evidence to indicate that this is the case for all children.[10] Various studies suggest that something in the order of 1% of pretend play develops into real aggression, although this does rise to 25% in children who are socially marginalized or have aggressive tendencies, suggesting that for them other types of play may be more appropriate.[11]

As always, it is a matter of balance. In the same way that a great big lump of salt is bad for you, particularly if you have weak kidneys, so an overemphasis on play that involves weapons and destruction can colour a boy's view of the world and his interaction with other children and adults. But just as a light sprinkling of salt enhances the flavour of the other foods that you are eating, perhaps a freedom to engage in 'war play' and 'superhero games' can feed the imagination and develop an interest in other activities and areas of play.

Muscular Christianity

In the second half of the nineteenth century a phenomenon now called 'Muscular Christianity' developed. Picking up on the ideas of writers like Rousseau,[12] many Victorians were exploring the relationship between sport, physical fitness and religion and believed that participation in sport could contribute to the development of Christian morality and 'manly' character. In our postmodern culture, a misogynistic view that sees manliness as compatible with godliness and as an 'antidote to the poison of effeminacy'[13] perhaps does not sit well, but I am disinclined to side entirely with E. M. Forster who suggests that those educated in this way end up with 'well developed bodies . . . and underdeveloped hearts'.[14] In the church setting where my research was carried out, more girls than boys expressed a preference for 'running around games' and I do not believe that wishing to express themselves physically means that they are at risk from underdeveloping emotionally.

While not denying that an overemphasis on physical prowess can limit spiritual and emotional development, particularly if a boy feels physically unable to match up to his peers' or his own expectations, I would like to see further exploration of how sport and physical activity can be a way for boys to engage with and express their spirituality.

Frosh and his research colleagues discovered that 'popular masculinity' involves sporting prowess as well as 'hardness' and 'coolness', and that boys spend a great deal of energy differentiating themselves from girls in this way.[15] They also discovered (perhaps not surprisingly) that football was a key motif in the boys' constructions of masculinities. I have to say I am not a fan of football, but I am fascinated by the religious fervour that it creates, and intrigued that when I talk to male children's and youth workers about whether football might be a 'spiritual connection' not one of them disagrees and many immediately light up with the possibilities. For years we have known that the best way to get children (and in particular boys) to come to our clubs is to take a ball to the green outside, and there are a number of organizations using football (amongst other sports) as a vehicle for evangelism,[16] but how can we go further than that and use football, or indeed any sport, as a means of helping children to engage with their spirituality?

It is interesting that, when responding to the 'I feel . . .' posters, while some of the children indicated sports (including football) as something which helped them to feel closer to God, or that they mattered or belonged, the number was not as significant as might be expected (although at one X:site, six boys did say that they felt they belonged because of membership of a team). The challenge to us, then, is this: why, when on a Sunday morning our playing fields are full of children and young people taking part in sport, are they not relating this to their spiritual well-being? The obvious reply is that those who answered the question are not on the pitch on a Sunday morning, they are in church. But does that not simply raise further questions? How do we encourage those who are in church to engage with God through more aspects of their lives? And for those on the pitch, how can we encourage them to see that some of their experiences there have a connection with the teachings of the church? If we want boys to connect with God, we first of all have to connect with them where they are, and that may well be on the football pitch.

On driving past the Southend United home ground, I was intrigued to see that it is decorated with an enormous lighted picture of a bunch of players piled on top of each other in what can only be described as a 'celebratory cuddle'. This would indicate to me that for whoever commissioned the sign, and for whoever designed it, the emphasis is not on the skill of scoring, but on the camaraderie of winning. Perhaps football is not just about being good with a ball – it is also about being part of a team and achieving something together.

Have we missed a trick here in our children's and youth work? Are we sometimes so focused on 'training' our children to 'score' properly that we forget to encourage them in the camaraderie of having already 'won' the greatest prize of all, the unconditional love of God?

The importance of touch

More than that, I think the Southend United sign gives us another clue to the reason why sport and rough play is such an important part of the lives of many boys and young men. It is all about touch. For those who perhaps struggle to articulate how they are feeling, a manly bundle on the pitch says it all; for those who question their value in the scheme of things, a slap on the back from a teammate brings the knowledge of belonging; and for those who wonder at the 'otherness' of creation, a congratulatory hug brings it into perspective.

I ran a group for eleven- to fourteen-year-olds for many years, and always joked that it was like running two groups. On one side of the room I had a gathering of girls, desperately trying to appear elegant and sophisticated. On the other side of the room I had a writhing pile of boys. Both groups were engaged in the business of trying to work out their identities, make sense of their lives and find out where they belonged. The girls were tending to do this verbally, and the boys were tending to do this physically.

If boys are not getting the sense of belonging they crave from appropriate touch, then where are they going to find it? Could it be that the increasing violence on the streets is an indication that they are finding it in ways that are not helpful to themselves and others? Just watch a group of drunk young men and you will see how, with their inhibitions reduced, they are much more likely to use touch as a form of communication (both positive and negative). The downside of child protection legislation is, I fear, that we are becoming less willing to touch children. My belief is that boys need that touch almost more than girls, and will go out of their way to find it. I know that whenever we are at church, I do not need to search for my nine-year-old son – he can always be found dangling from our long-suffering male youth worker. What a fantastic opportunity we have as God's family on earth to offer children, and in particular boys, positive contact with adults.

 So how . . . do we encourage boys to engage with and express their spirituality through play and touch?

Permission to play

If play is the work of the boys you have in your group, in what ways do you give or withhold permission to do that? What flexibility can you add to your programme that provides them with opportunities for free play and the resources to carry this out? At the Scripture Union Mission of which I am a part, our afternoon programme is made up of craft and game workshops that the children can choose to do. A couple of years ago we started a 'free play' workshop, where we provided sand, water, cars and so on. It worked really well. One of my most cherished moments is coming into the church and watching one five-year-old boy playing with a car. After a couple of vrooms, he would send it off down the length of the church carpet and, as he watched, sitting on his bottom, he would wave both his arms and his legs in sheer joy. This action became for many of us a symbol of what it is to be a child, totally and utterly caught up in the moment, but I think that there are a couple of other things we can learn from this. For this boy, who lived in a small house with two older brothers, the space – both physical and mental – to play in this way was of considerable importance. It is easy to be discouraged by our large, cold, draughty buildings, but perhaps if we look at them through the eyes of a child we might see them as Aladdin's caves of play opportunities.

Football feelings

If sport is such a big part of the lives of many of our boys, how can we help them to relate that to their faith and spirituality? Below are some starter questions you can use to help them reflect on what it means to them and how it can connect them with God.

- What difference does being a fan make to you?
- What things do you do / have that help you to feel you belong to the club?
- How do you feel about being part of a team?
- What relationships within that team help you to know who you are?
- What is it like to win?
- How do your heart, mind and body feel while you are running around the pitch with your shirt over your head having just scored the winning goal?
- What sense of the ultimate and all-powerful are you tapping into?
- What does it feel like to lose?
- What makes losing feel better?
- What makes losing feel worse?
- What can be learned from this?

Warriors and heroes

The Bible is full of battles – some that, to us in our post-modern Western world, seem gratuitous, others that are symbolic of the battle of good against evil. Are we willing to get out of our comfort zone and let our boys pretend that they are in Joshua's army, or pushing down the temple like Samson? And if we are, what mechanisms can we use to help them to think about why it happened and what it means for them? The list of questions in the 'Football feelings' section above can easily be adjusted for use in a discussion after a battle re-enactment or similar activity. Equally, a quiet piece of music and an opportunity to reflect might be appropriate, depending on the story in which they have taken part.

Rough and tumble

Children love adults who are willing to play,[17] and it is through this spontaneity that we are able to build relationships and create that sense of connection with others that is so important in many definitions of spirituality. Speaking at the Children Matter Forum in 2009, Peter Jeffrey, National Chairman of Urban Saints, who has been leading boys' groups for many years, gave lots of evidence of the power of 'rough and tumble' in his ministry. He believes that the opportunities to wrestle and play robust games have a huge impact on the boys' sense of belonging and willingness to engage with other more 'religious' activities.

What games can we play that do not promote aggressiveness, but allow children and adults appropriate physical contact? I have recently discovered the delights of Tag Rugby,[18] a fast-moving sport that reduces the risk of little people getting squashed by bigger ones. And of course you can do just about anything three-legged, if you put your mind to it!

Boys only

There is still much debate about whether we should be offering our children single-sex groups, and there are persuasive arguments on either side. Having seen the evidence from my eleven- to fourteen-year-olds, and heard Peter Jeffrey's stories from Urban Saints, I am increasingly convinced that we should be offering boys and girls the opportunities to meet sometimes in single-sex groups and engage in activities and conversations in which they might feel inhibited if there were members of the opposite sex present.

Be aware

If you are working with boys who are on the autistic spectrum, then you will know that touch can be a more significant issue for them. As one of the symptoms of the condition is a different way of processing stimulation to the senses, children with autism may suffer from hyper- (too much) or hypo- (too little) sensitivity to different stimulations. A boy with hyper-sensitivity to sound will not be able to cope with noisy games, whereas one with hyposensitivity may need to make repetitive noises or tap things to make them vibrate, in order to reassure himself of his presence in the world. Equally you may find that one boy cannot bear to be touched – describing it as painful – while another finds firm pressure comforting and helpful. Again, it is down to knowing the child, and working closely with the parents and other professionals responsible for his care.

Things to think about

- If you are a parent, and particularly a dad, how much time do you spend wrestling with your sons?
- How much 'free play' are you allowing the children as part of your 'programme'?
- Do you have team members who are willing and able to engage in appropriate 'rough play' with the children?
- Have you made all the necessary legal checks and called references for all your team members so that you are happy that they are safe to engage in appropriate 'rough play'?
- Where are your own boundaries on aggressive / rough / gun play? Why are those boundaries where they are? Do they need to shift?
- Can you offer the boys an opportunity to meet together as 'boys only', perhaps once a term?

3. ONCE UPON A TIME
STORY

'Once upon a time there were three bears . . . ' Bouncing around in the back of the ambulance, I gripped my three-year-old daughter's hand. ' . . . There was a Daddy bear, and a Mummy bear, and a Baby bear . . . ' Her big brown eyes stared at me over the oxygen mask. ' . . . One day the Mummy bear decided to make some porridge for breakfast . . . ' I glanced at the swelling in her neck: the offending two pence piece that she had swallowed was now stuck, severely restricting her breathing and swallowing. 'Keep her awake!' they had said to me at our local Accident & Emergency department as they sent us off for this forty-minute ride to the nearest Ear, Nose and Throat department. ' . . . But the porridge was too cold . . . ' Her eyes flashed at me. It had worked: she might not be able to talk, but she was telling me I had got it wrong. ' . . . Ah no, the porridge wasn't too cold, it was too hot. So Daddy bear, Mummy bear and Baby bear went for a walk while it cooled down . . . ' 'Blues and Twos!' the shout came from the front of the ambulance, as the *sirens wailed into action to get us through the traffic. 'Oh God, please don't take her away.' The anaesthetist who had to accompany us just in case she stopped breathing and had to be operated on en route nudged me. 'Keep going,' he said. ' . . . Meanwhile, through the woods, came a girl with hair that shone like gold. In fact, it was so beautiful that people called her Goldilocks . . . ' The story went on. Each time she seemed to be slipping into unconsciousness, I deliberately got it wrong, smiling and twinkling at her as her eyes refocused saying, 'Silly Mummy!' On the inside I was crying out to God from the depths of my soul; on the outside the story finished with a much more happily ever after than normal, and we made it to the hospital. Miraculously, just as they were prepping her for theatre, she did a great big hiccup and started talking. X-rays proved that the coin had moved. She was going to be OK. ' . . . And the Daddy bear and Mummy bear and Baby bear all lived happily ever after, even if Mummy bear had to sift poo for two weeks to make sure the coin had reached its final destination . . . '*

In his autobiographical account of his early childhood, French philosopher Jean-Paul Sartre says, 'A man is always a teller of stories. He lives surrounded by his own stories and those of other people.'[1] All of us have stories to tell, all of us are programmed to listen to the stories of others, so why is it that sometimes we limit 'stories' to the recounting of well-known nursery tales? One of the findings of the Biblos Project, a Bible Society research project into children and the Bible, was that 'narrative' was considered a more helpful term than 'story' because it seemed less 'fictional'. What a shame that we no longer appear to recognize the richness of story and its importance in our lives.

There are three aspects that are significant in helping us to understand how fundamental story is, not just to our cognitive development, but also to our sense of well-being and to our meaning-making. The first aspect is the understanding that we have our own story, the highs and lows, characters and patterns that shape who we are. The second is that, as Christians, we have a part in God's story. The third aspect is the importance of story in helping children give expression to emotions and work through different situations, which they may or may not have come across themselves, through the experience of another.

Some research into spirituality,[2] although not specifically looking for gender differences, does focus on the idea of personal narrative, a concept that may be more readily expressed by a girl than by a boy. However, boys are quite capable of following the complex plot of *Doctor Who*, and one of the acclamations of the '*Harry Potter* phenomenon' was that it was getting a lot of boys reading. Boys *are* able to systemize the events of their lives – but it is probably the expression of this personal narrative that they find more difficult, and stories can help them do that. Anderson and Foley, in their wonderful book called *Mighty Stories, Dangerous Rituals*, believe that each child is born into a web of stories, myths and legends, many of which carry both implicitly and explicitly the expectations of that child's family and culture.[3] Their stories will include the nature of their conception and birth; the quirks and traits of their parents and grandparents; the feuds and loyalties of the extended family and community in which they live. As the child grows, so their web of stories becomes more complex, and this is one of the reasons why children often ask, 'Do you remember when . . . ?' In this they are asking us to help them clarify and ratify their experiences and understanding. For boys this is particularly important. As they systemize the data, we do not want them to lose the meaning or emotion that accompanies it. What is essential is that we listen carefully, and respond accurately, to the stories that they share with us, ensuring that we not only get the story straight, but that we connect with their understanding of the story, and perhaps hear the story beneath the surface.

It has been suggested that as human beings we are pro-grammed for verbal rather than written communication,[4] and that literacy is a product of cultural conditioning. Evidence from national tests indicates that girls are more successful at literacy than boys, and that boys are more likely to be less experienced readers than girls and less confident writers.[5] Is it fair, then, to expect them to engage with their spirituality through a medium that they feel neither comfortable with nor competent in? Certainly the boys at X:site did not really see writing something down as helpful. Berryman argues that there has been an overemphasis on text in Western culture, which has masked the importance of oral communication.[6] He reminds us that the two most influential individuals in Western philosophical thought have been Socrates and Jesus Christ, neither of whom, he says, are recorded as having written anything down. In fact, Jesus' parable about the two builders[7] indicates that he is far more interested in listening that becomes action than in learning that becomes clever literature.

Through story we can offer boys a source of 'connatural knowing', or innate understanding, giving them the opportunity to *encounter* God and make sense of their lives in a way that is relevant to them. I love the story that Mike Yaconelli describes that has us watch a young child leaning over the edge of her younger brother's pram or cot. She is whispering to him, 'Tell me what God sounds like; I am starting to forget.'[8] As children hear the stories in the Bible and hear the stories of God's action in the lives of people around them, it will resonate with what they already know deep in their spirit to be true.

The importance of imagination

Some believe that by offering children fantasy stories we are in danger of encouraging them to dismiss the stories that we believe to be true, or of helping them to fashion a view of life for themselves that avoids reality. I believe, however, that the danger of squashing a boy's imagination, or of not giving him the opportunity to develop his empathy and understanding of conflicting emotions and difficult situations, is far greater. As the characters in the story he is reading or hearing encounter love, loyalty, dishonesty and disappointment, so he encounters them in a manner that does him no harm, and instead helps him to start to make his own sense of these themes of life. Other writers have demonstrated the importance of fairy tales in revealing to children the existence of evil in a way they can absorb without trauma.[9] My worry with the creation of films from books is that children are now exposed to monsters that they did not have to face directly when reading or listening to a story. Many boys have extremely effective imaginations. When you are imagining a story, you know the monster is there, but you do not have to look at it directly. In a film you cannot avoid it, and therefore we have to be careful what we allow our boys to see.

Plenty of writers believe that narrative and ritual are the means by which we not only discover meaning for ourselves, but also communicate it to others.[10] Smith and Shortt, in their helpful book *The Bible and the Task of Teaching It*,[11] suggest that the importance of understanding this is being rediscovered by educators and biblical scholars, and they argue that much can be learned when we see the Bible as a narrative rather than as something to be immediately translated into doctrine. My experience as a storyteller concurs with the view that stories enable both the teller and the listener to enter into the experience, being drawn into it through both internal and external dimensions and being made aware of what have been described as its 'energized aspects'.[12] I once watched my father hand a child listening to his story an imaginary pot to hold. Entranced, she cradled the pot in her hands as the story unfolded and she learned the importance of its contents. When the time came, she handed it back with all due care and reverence. For both the storyteller and the listener this pot was 'real' because the story was alive and happening around them.

Story creating dialogue

Stories allow us to hold contradictions in tension in a way that perhaps straight dialogue does not. Children are often very aware of these contradictions and the perplexing nature of societal rules and norms. For some boys, and perhaps for children who are on the autistic spectrum, this can be a frustrating problem – when things are neither wrong nor right, not one thing or another, but hang instead somewhere in the middle dependent on varying circumstances. This is why I think that stories and 'wondering' can be particularly helpful for boys who, perhaps, more naturally incline to a right or wrong answer, and get anxious when they cannot see their way towards this. By gently questioning assumptions and allowing an authentic dialogue, we can help boys to philosophize and make sense and meaning in their lives.

The Godly Play method of storytelling involves the teller learning a carefully worded script and making no eye contact at all with the listeners. The idea is that the teller, as well as the listener, is 'in' the story. One of the advantages of this particular storytelling style is that it does have positive implications for the power relations in the exchange: the children as listeners are on a more equal footing with the adult, who is usually the teller. I do, however, have some concerns with the level of non-interaction that happens during this type of story-telling. If we perceive a narrative to be an organic thing, that grows and changes with the telling and the interaction between the participants, then such a scripted event might curtail some of those 'energized aspects'. Nonetheless, this non-interaction is overcome, to a certain extent, by the opportunity the children are given to ponder the story, with the 'I wonder . . . ' questions at the end.

God's story

The Bible is a narrative that displays the ups and downs of life in a rich and compelling way, but are we communicating this in a manner that is relevant to boys? Many years ago I read a book called *Offering the Gospel to Children*,[13] which funda-mentally changed my attitude to using the Bible with children. In it, the author warns against creating a 'kiddie gospel' with only the 'nice' bits of the Bible, saying that it does a disservice to children who already know that life is not nice. If we allow boys to 'wonder' about the biblical narrative and 'play' with the text, they will see the issues raised by it at the level at which they are able to see. This is one of the reasons why Joseph is such a great story to use in schools. We use it as part of our Year 6 transition programme because it starts with a blended family, deals with jealousy, bullying and unfairness, and has a smattering of violence and a hint of sex! This story finishes with a happy ending, but we should not be frightened of using stories that do not, as we learn together about God's faithfulness.

The Bible is full of stories of battles – in fact it has more sex, blood and violence than Shakespeare! Are we in danger of sanitizing a story that is full of the reality of humanity? A few years ago I was asked at the last minute to lead a session with eight- to eleven-year-olds based on 1 Kings 18. I explained to the group that in a moment we would act out the story, but while they were finishing their refreshments I would read it to them from the Bible. I read the passage, trying to put as much excitement and action into it as I could, and convey the power of God through his ability to make a soaking wet altar burst into flames. As I got to the end of the passage the defeated prophets of Baal ran down to the river where they were captured, and as I turned the page it dawned on me what was going to happen next. Reading ahead, I spotted that all of them were then seriously massacred. In a nanosecond I considered my options. I could stop there – capturing was, after all, quite sufficient – or I could continue. I decided to hold my nerve and read on, thereby living out my belief that we should not create a 'kiddie gospel' and that children need to understand the Bible in its entirety. As I closed the book, twelve pairs of eyes gazed at me in stunned silence, until one of the boys piped up, 'But I thought you said that God said we weren't supposed to kill people.' What then ensued was the most amazing conversation which covered sin, heaven, hell and predestination – a conversation which probably would not have happened if I had bottled out and finished with a nice neat capture!

For the RE lessons in the research project, conducted with two classes, I tested the children's responses to two different storytelling techniques: a Godly Play style story which involved moving across a large piece of green felt characters that represented the people of Israel leaving Egypt and receiving the Ten Commandments; and in a different lesson some 'dialling down' techniques that included deep breathing, followed by listening to a story being read. The children had obviously never seen anything like the Godly Play before, and it took them a while to settle. Eventually, after they realized that I was not engaging with them but concentrating on the story, they also concentrated on what was going on, on the felt mat. One girl, diagnosed with ADHD,[14] found it especially hard to focus, and I had to resist the urge to lift my head and make eye contact with her, even though I believed this may have helped her to become more engaged. The boy to my left also found it rather entertaining to move the little plastic frogs I had used to represent the plagues into inappropriate positions, which was distracting to say the least!

What is really interesting is that when it came to the 'wondering', the statistics show that the boys found it much more helpful than the girls. For the first class, the focus – predominantly from the girls – was on the co-dependency of the commandments, and the fact that all of them are important. In the second class, the discussion quickly moved on to the

RE lesson data: response to storytelling activities

	Boys in favour	Girls in favour
I enjoyed watching the story unfold	91%	88%
Listening to and watching the story helped me think about what was being said	65%	65%
Wondering about the story helped me to think about what it meant to me	43%	24%
I enjoyed listening to the stories	80%	38%
Using my imagination helped me to think about what was being said	55%	43%

subject of honouring your parents. At the time the case of 'Baby P' was being discussed widely in the press and the boys were obviously wrestling with this. This particular method-ology gave them an opportunity to explore an issue that mattered to them in a safe way.

Both genders obviously found the story they could watch as well as hear more helpful than one they simply had to listen to, but it is interesting that the boys still enjoyed just listening, and were able to engage with the 'sense- and meaning-making' using both techniques. This data, and the fact that 'listening to someone telling a Bible story' was the fifth most popular way to hear from God amongst the boys at X:site, indicates clearly just how important stories are to boys, and how crucial it is to give them time to process them.

 So how . . . do we help boys to engage with and express their spirituality through story?

Are you sitting comfortably? Then I'll begin . . .

At the end of each afternoon of games and workshops at our Family Mission, we have what we call a 'bedtime story'. The children settle down at the feet of someone sitting in a comfy chair, who then reads them a story from a book. The pictures are projected on a screen behind them so that no-one has to strain to see them. The children are always entranced, and there is very little fidgeting, if any. The books are not often Christian (although we have enjoyed the Punchinello series[15]), but have some kind of message to help the children think about their life. There is no explanation or application, just story.

Although it can be a time-consuming process to scan the pictures and crop them so that they work well as part of a

PowerPoint presentation, it is, I think, worth the effort. If you are thinking of doing it, please make sure you contact the publisher first and ask for permission to copy and project the pictures. Sometimes it takes a few weeks for permission to come through, so it is worth thinking about this well in advance!

'I wonder . . . '

Sometimes we can be guilty of over-explaining a story or parable. It is a tendency which not only underestimates a child's ability to connect with a narrative in a way beyond reasoning, but can also, perhaps more worryingly, diminish the child's sense of wonder and awe, and demystify the mystery of God. Sometimes we need to have the courage to let the story speak for itself. The beauty of the 'I wonder' questions used in Godly Play – such as, 'I wonder which bit of the story is your favourite?' or, 'I wonder which bit of the story could be left out, and not change it?' – is that they allow boys time to think through the story and ponder its meaning for themselves without worrying that there has to be a right or wrong answer. Sometimes this requires us to hold our nerve, as we mediate the 'less helpful' comments and give time for the deeper thinking to rise to the surface.

I'm listening

Stories have power to speak to everyone. Sometimes we can fall into the trap of thinking that we are the ones who are dispensing wisdom to others, and we forget that we, as the storyteller, are 'in the story' too and need to allow it to speak to us. I remember on one occasion being right in the middle of a story during an assembly when I realized that what I was saying was also for me to hear. The story was about Abraham and God's faithfulness, and there was a recurring phrase that was threaded through the story. It added structure and rhythm to the storytelling. About the third time I said it, it was almost as if my internal ears had opened for the first time and I realized just what truth that simple phrase had for me. Without putting ourselves at risk of bursting into tears and being unable to continue, we need to be open to what the story has to say. If we are not 'listening', then how can we expect our boys to 'listen' too?

Let me tell you a story

Encourage the children to tell their own stories. Mark Yaconelli describes a simple ritual that helps adults and young people to 'focus' at the start of a meeting.[16] The same technique can be used with boys to help them share their stories. Sitting in a circle, take it in turns to hold an egg-timer while you share the story of something that happened during your day or week. When the sand runs out, it is time to pass the timer on for the next story. This technique could also be adjusted for use around the tea table at home.

In his book about the science of story, Kendall Haven talks about 'the blanket myth – everything is a story'.[17] Everything is not a story, but it can become one. As the children practise sharing their news, we can model storytelling to them. Not that we are encouraging them to lie, but instead we are encouraging them to make meaning of their life events. If a story is 'a detailed, character-based narration of a character's struggles to overcome obstacles and reach an important goal',[18] then there is no need to fabricate an encounter in the playground or at home. Their lives are full of character-based struggles: all they need to do is frame it in a way that engages our sense of wonder and meaning-making. For those who are natural storytellers this will come easily (which is where the egg-timer comes into its own!). Others may need encouragement, and help with the 'wondering' at what has happened in their lives.

Show me a story

The benefits of using pictures and props as part of storytelling have been illustrated above, but for those boys who struggle with reading, picture Bibles are particularly helpful. When Jeff Anderson illustrated *The Lion Graphic Bible*, he deliberately chose to portray a Jesus who is rugged and much more 'manly' than traditional pictures to which children are often exposed. The deep colours and picture style also have a 'comic strip' feel that is attractive to boys, and gets them into the story perhaps without them really realizing it. Scripture Union have also produced 'Bible Comic' materials with boys in mind.

Revise the vocab

I do have concerns that more and more children do not have any religious or spiritual vocabulary, and agree with the view that much of the language, symbols and rituals of the Christian story are losing plausibility in our culture.[19] Stories can help us to redress the balance and give our boys the vocabulary they need to express their faith and spirituality. Stories need rhythm and pattern, and it is therefore very easy to explain a term without actually explaining it, by saying the same thing in two different ways, one after the other. In this way boys can be introduced to words that will help them consider and explain their own spirituality, without feeling that they are being 'taught' religious language.

Things to think about

- How do you relay the story of your life?
- Who are the storytellers and actors in your church or team or family? How can you encourage and enhance this gift?
- Who are the storytellers amongst your children? How can you use this gift to help the others engage with their own stories?
- Have you created a 'kiddie gospel'? Do you need to revisit God's story so that you can share it with the children more comprehensively?

4. MAKE IT GO AWAY
PAIN AND LOSS

It was four o'clock in the morning. Her brain couldn't work out what that noise was, or why she was suddenly so awake. And then she realized. It was her son, whimpering in pain. Lurching to her feet, she stumbled to the kitchen to get the pink medicine, without even opening her eyes. Back on his half of the corner sofa, the pain-stiffened boy guzzled the medicine and let her stroke his head for a bit before returning to a fitful sleep. They had done this for pretty much twenty-four hours, after a routine operation had gone wrong and left him with some very painful wounds. As she returned to her half of the sofa, desperate to be asleep again, she tried to pray but could feel no connection. She laughed inwardly to herself. 'Why would there be?' This was not spiritual, it sucked!

It was Robert Coles, in his book *The Spiritual Life of Children*,[1] who first alerted me to the idea that pain and loss may be a 'spiritual connection'. He suggested that bereavement, or physical pain, may actually create an unusual psychological arousal and connect with a person's 'spiritual inwardness' as the sufferer is prompted to examine his or her past, present and future. Other writers, perhaps not surprisingly, also suggest that many spiritual experiences cited are related in some way to death or catastrophic events.[2] There is a peculiar intimacy about pain and loss. Physically, we may need to do more things for a child than previously, and as we do, the way that we touch them can have an important restorative power, as through it they sense their value and belonging. Emotionally, a child may be unable to feel anything in an initial numbness, and then the rawness of the emotion can make them very vulnerable. It is at these times that adults and children can draw comfort from each other as they live through a similar experience. Spiritually, a child may be more conscious of the relationship between people, the world and 'other' and may be much more questioning of previously held beliefs as they ask the bigger questions, such as, 'Why is this happening to me?'

By saying that 'pain and loss' can be a spiritual connection, I am not suggesting that inflicting pain or loss on a boy is a route to enhancing his spirituality, but rather that we accept that pain or loss might actually be part of his journey and it is our role to help him explore this. Of course, deep trauma can have a terrible and long-lasting effect on a child, and we must do everything in our power to prevent the trauma and to relieve a child's pain, confusion and suffering. But my argument is that part of that process is to identify and encourage those moments when he is more aware of his relationship to others, and where he can start to unravel what has happened to him in the spiritual as well as the emotional domain.

To test 'pain and loss' as a 'spiritual connection' properly would have required carefully planned interviews carried out by those qualified and experienced in this area, and this was not appropriate for my particular research project. There were, however, snippets that the children shared on the 'I feel . . .' posters and during discussions in the RE lessons that showed this was a significant area for them. For instance, in the question-and-answer session in Lesson Three and the 'wondering' at the end of Lesson Four, many of the comments from the boys indicated that they were wrestling with pain and loss, not necessarily always their own, but also that which they see in the world around them. On the 'I feel . . .' posters, a number of children, and in particular the boys, said that they felt closest to God when they were feeling unhappy or left out, indicating that for them emotional vulnerability led them to seek assurance and comfort in the spiritual as well as the physical realm.

Boys feel things deeply, but factors like vocabulary and peer pressure mean that they might not share those things in the same ways as girls do. As a result, what started as the pain of rejection or bereavement then becomes the secondary emotion of anger, and their behaviour can become aggressive and/or attention-seeking. One little boy I know, whose family situation means that he is always competing for attention at home, is a delight when he is getting one-to-one attention, but as soon as he is with other children, he resorts to attention-seeking behaviour. It is very hard not to get frustrated with the constant distraction when you are running a large group and one child is proving difficult, but what we need to remember is that somewhere behind that behaviour is likely to be some deeply felt pain. Our job is to continue to be firm but fair, but also to provide opportunities for such children to explore that pain and pathways through it.

So how . . . do we encourage boys to engage with and express their spirituality through pain and loss?

How much does it hurt?

A child in hospital with a dislocated elbow was asked to describe the level of pain, with 1 being no pain and 10 being the world's worst pain. The answer '2' did not seem to make sense, as it was clear that the injury was very severe. On further questioning, it turned out that the child had taken literally the phrase 'the world's worst pain' and had compared what she was feeling to what it must feel like to lose your family in a flood or earthquake, or starve to death. Needless to say, she soon got the pain relief she needed!

Pain is relative. Children who have suffered a great deal can become quite stoical about pain, while others who have never really been hurt can make a great deal of fuss about something quite minor. Some people believe the rhyme, 'Sticks and stones can break my bones, but names can never hurt me.' Others of us are wounded beyond measure by the thoughtless words of others. When we are journeying alongside children who are in physical or emotional pain, the best thing that we can do to help them start to make sense of it and find a way through it is to accept that it hurts and give them opportunities to express that.

Tell me the story

You too may have been struck by how, after an operation or serious trauma, some boys are keen to tell their story. When visitors arrive and ask how he is, he may well launch into a chronologically correct and vivid account of what has happened to him. If you listen carefully, you will realize that what is happening is part of the healing process for him. In a situation where he has been in extreme pain or fear, and where things have gone wrong and seemed out of control, he probably felt bewildered and vulnerable. By telling the story he is taking control, connecting again with those moments of extreme emotion, and trying to make sense and meaning from it.

When boys arrive at our activities wanting to tell us about their story of pain and loss, we need to be ready to stop and listen. If they arrive not sure how to start that story, we need to be ready to help them by asking questions, or by giving them play opportunities that can trigger the right kind of conversation. Sand, water and liquid cornflour are all media that can give boys a 'blank canvas' to work with. For small boys, doctors' kits or toy ambulances and fire engines may be the vehicles for their expression.

As parents, we need to be patient and allow him to speak for himself. It does not matter if details are not correct or sensations are exaggerated. If he is telling his story to someone else, it is our privilege to be listening in, not our duty to make it factually correct. And if we are worried that he is not telling his story, can we invite round someone he trusts, who might just be the catalyst for some kind of healing expression?

Tightly and lightly

Pain and loss can be very debilitating, and require us to rely very heavily on others. For children it can be very confusing and frustrating as they may no longer be capable of the skills they feel they have so recently mastered. It might be something physical like going to the toilet, it might be something emotional like bursting into tears at the smallest thing. For boys this can be particularly difficult to cope with, as their vulnerability can, in some cases, make them feel emasculated and thereby double the anguish and frustration. It is a great honour to be asked to come alongside somebody in this situation, and we must hold their vulnerability securely but lightly. Trust, one of the foundational elements of sound faith development, is key. We need to be reliable, but also in tune with their recuperation and growing health. Sometimes we need to be gently nudging them to try to do something for themselves, or to see things in a new way, just as a horse noses her newborn foal into walking. But above all, as we see new signs of growth and health, we must be prepared to step back more and more, and not create a dependency that might make us feel needed but does not really meet the needs of the child for whom we are caring.

Tangible evidence

Rituals are very important for boys, particularly when pain and loss are making everything else in their life feel out of control, and this is where you might see small OCDs[3] creep into their behaviour. What rituals and patterns can you use as part of your work with boys that can free them up rather than shut them down? Interest is increasing in 'modern monasticism' and the effect of daily patterns of prayer and worship.[4] Think about the daily, weekly, monthly patterns and structures you can put in place for your boys, to give them security and order. What things of beauty can you show them and surround them with to lift their souls beyond the physicality of their pain, if only momentarily, into awe and wonder?

If you have ever spent any time on a hospital ward, you may have noticed how quickly children and their families territorialize their space. By putting up cards and so on, they are trying to make tangible the intangible experience they are going through, and represent the network of belonging from which they are removed, if only temporarily. Something as simple as a card made by a group of which he is a part can be significant in helping a boy in pain know that he belongs, or a familiar object brought from home can remind him of a place of safety and security and his connection with others.

Rites of passage

All the time, boys are experiencing minor losses as they make a transition from one stage to another. What rites of passage can you introduce to help your boys 'say goodbye' to one part of their life and welcome another? Photos of first days at school, or a first toothy gap, are important for parents, but also for the children themselves. If they are able to see the landmarks and their value to those who love them, then perhaps they will not mourn their passing quite so deeply. Take photos of your group. Prepare scrapbooks of their time with you, or even adopt the American tradition of yearbooks that include pictures of all the group members.

As a family, what simple rituals can you put in place for your boys to look forward to, to mark their transition to the next stage of their life? What traditions surround their special day and show their value and belonging? In our family, you get a front door key for your eleventh birthday, a symbol of freedom and autonomy.

Be real

Not long after my friend died, I was doing an RE lesson. It was one of my favourite types of lessons, where the children have made up questions and you get to talk about all sorts of areas of your faith. In this session one child asked me whether I ever got angry with God. Instantly I had the pat answer in my head ready to deliver, but that was not the truth. I *was* cross with God for taking away my friend and leaving her children motherless, and to say otherwise was to diminish me and him. And so I explained to the children that I was furious with God for what had happened, and wanted to scream and shout like a toddler, but just as I would pick up my children when they had tantrums, and hold them and hold them and tell them how much I loved them until they stopped, so God was holding and holding me, and telling me how much he loved me, until somehow the pain and the anger subsided. Boys know the world is a wonderful and awful place, and this is why the Bible is such a good book for them, because it talks about the realities of betrayal, bereavement, deceit and anger. If we really want them to grow in their spirituality, then we must celebrate and wonder at the wonderful, but we must also acknowledge the awful.

Imagine

The world can be a very frightening place, and I think that children have far greater access to frightening images than they ever had before. When I was a child, although we were never burgled, I was very scared of burglars. I would spend what seemed like many hours during the night lying flat out under the covers, practising not breathing, so that if a burglar came in he would not notice that I was there! I wish I had possessed the foresight that my son showed in asking Mummy to come in with her 'sonic screwdriver' and get rid of anything that was scary. The imagination can be used to help boys overcome some elements of their pain and fear, and to see a way through that helps them to make sense and meaning of it all. Stories and games that offer escapism are important, but we do need to be aware of those children who are using their imagination as a permanent escape from something in the real world from which they actually need to be rescued.

Ready to play

Just because children are caught in the middle of a major catastrophe or traumatic event does not mean that they should not or cannot play. A boy whose parents are grieving might feel guilty that all he wants to do is run around outside with a ball. It is not that he does not care or feel acutely his own pain or that of others. It is just that his approach to it is not the approach or experience of an adult, and it should not be treated as such. Sometimes our role as children's worker, friend or parent is to give children opportunities to play despite the situation in which they find themselves.

Get help

There are now some online resources with ideas for helping children express their feelings of pain and loss.[5] If one of your boys has experienced a major bereavement or is going through a serious illness or parental divorce, then you might feel that he needs more professional help. Sometimes it is difficult to talk to the parents, but a phone call to the school might help in either raising the issue, or finding out that they are already dealing with it. Of course, if a child makes a disclosure of abuse, then you must follow your agency's policy to get the necessary help.

Things to think about

- What kinds of pain and loss do you know your boys have experienced / are experiencing?
- What connections do you have with local agencies that can support children with specific needs? How can you make or strengthen these connections?
- Would it be worth someone in your team exploring further training on working with children who are traumatized by divorce or bereavement?

5. POO, BUM, WILLY
HUMOUR

When I went to look around our current house with a view to buying it, I was greeted at the door by a very excited eight-year-old boy, shortly followed by his mother and sister. They went to our church, so there was the usual exchange of news and pleasantries before the tour of the house. This young man took his role very seriously. Not only did he point out the star features of the house, like the fact that you could jump from the banisters onto the sofa, and the dent in the airing cupboard door caused by a fight between him and his sister, but he also entertained me by telling me a rude joke in every room we went into. As I stared out of the window, in what is now my daughter's room, desperately trying not to laugh, I could feel behind me the strain and desperation of his mother as once again he launched into another joke which inevitably contained the words 'poo', 'bum' or 'willy'. Looking back on that day, knowing that both that eight-year-old boy and his sister are now fine Christian young people of whom I am very fond and proud, I wonder at what was going on. How exciting and terrifying it must have been for that boy. On the one hand, proud to show off his home to somebody from church, he wanted to offer something, a small gift. With nothing else at his disposal, the only offering he could make was to make me laugh – and the only jokes he could remember were rude! On the other hand, although he would have been told that he had a new home to go to, at eight he was still not yet able to fully rationalize the belief that if I bought his house, he would not be homeless. To cover his insecurity, he resorted to something that made him feel better – jokes that made him laugh.

I chose to include humour as a 'spiritual connection' despite the fact that it is largely ignored by the writers on spirituality I have studied. While I believe that children's spirituality is a subject that should be taken seriously, I do not think that it should be completely serious. Children seem to me to have an innate sense of humour and I wonder whether, for some, this is a means of connecting and meaning-making beyond the emotional and the physical. For centuries people have believed that laughter is the best medicine, and scientific research has now proved how humour makes people feel good by activating the brain reward areas, and reduces the effects of stress on the heart and immune system. Millar believes that the benefits go further than the physiological, and that humour loosens the ties to the ego and allows it to engage with the soul.[1] Certainly real laughter has no respect for dignity!

Cast your mind back to one of those moments when you have been helpless with laughter, particularly when you were not supposed to be, and see if you can remember the sense of unreality that it brought, the way nothing except the laughter really mattered, and the sense of being conspiratorially joined with those who were laughing too. See also if you can remember times when others were laughing about something and you did not know what it was. Did you find yourself laughing too, simply because it was infectious, or perhaps with a nervous laugh because you did not know what was going on? Or did you find yourself disapproving and feeling left out? There is commonality in laughter: when other people laugh, we laugh too. But there is also almost an anarchy about it that can make us feel very uncomfortable, particularly when it is inappropriate.

For boys, much of their humour revolves around bodily functions, hence the name of this chapter, and while I am not suggesting for a minute that we encourage them in lewdness, I think we need to pause before we shut down this type of humour. Sometimes as adults we forget the physicality of our world. Maybe I am being heretical by suggesting that Jesus may have laughed at bodily functions when he was a boy, but I would love to know whether it was part of God's design, or the fall, that created such an endless source of entertainment for boys! In the same way that war games may lead to other imaginative play, 'silly' humour may lead to a sense of release and cohesion in a group that endless discussions will never create.

Psychologists suggest that the repression of feelings, particularly those of anger and loss, can lead to all sorts of problems in adolescence. For boys, it appears that this is especially important as some of them struggle to pick up the skills required to express their feelings, as well as being under a great deal of pressure to assert their masculinity by avoiding all talk about feelings. Giving boys the opportunity to laugh together eases that tension. As humour also activates areas in the brain that respond to emotions, it may improve the boys' propensity to express other feelings as well, and thereby increase their sense of belonging and meaning, and help them to connect with God in new ways.

In the same way that it was difficult to intentionally test the impact of pain and loss on the children who participated in my research, it was also difficult to test humour without creating a false environment. (In *Young Masculinities*, humour was found to be very important for boys, so perhaps small discussion groups like those described in the book are the way to discover more about this.[2]) In the course of my research activities, humour was nonetheless evident in many of the responses from the children. In the Godly Play style story (see p. 79) there was great hilarity when the small frogs that represented the swarms were moved into all sorts of compromising positions by one boy, and when we tried to create our own percussion in one of the RE lessons, some of the children became quite helpless with laughter. At X:site, one of the boys responded, 'I feel closest to God when I am on the toilet.' Originally I thought that this was probably because it was the only place where he had time and space to ponder, but then, when I found similar writing that said 'I feel I belong when I am on the toilet' and 'I feel I matter when I am on the toilet', I began to think that it was possibly more an indication of this boy's humour than of his spirituality!

 So how . . . do we encourage boys to engage with and express their spirituality through humour?

Wiggly piggly words

For children, something is the funniest during the first months (maybe even a year or two) after the time it can first be understood.[3] The humour that your boys are using will be dependent on their age and cognitive development. Word play is an important part of humour for children throughout their verbal development, and for boys much of this involves getting words to sound as close to a rude word as possible, or simply inserting words like 'poo', 'bum' or 'willy' into sentences to see the effect. By allowing them to play with words and their meanings, we are helping them to open up neural paths that might otherwise take longer to develop. The key is once again knowing our boys well, so that we can discern when they are experimenting in a way that is helpful, and when they are being silly because they are bored.

See the funny side

Humour looks obliquely at things. One theory suggests that to make something a joke, rather than a logic puzzle or story, requires surprise, an ending that was not expected and is not necessarily the sensible outcome.[4] Looking obliquely at issues, experiences and stories can give us insights that we might not otherwise have had. Perhaps if we encourage boys when they see the funny side of things, and do not shut down their humorous exploration too soon, they might discover something new about the serious side of things too. We also need to think about the motives behind the humour. Is there some kind of insecurity being covered up, and if so, what can we do to alleviate it?

En-joy

Jesus came to give us life in all its fullness. Not necessarily so that our lives will become easier, but so that we can see the world in the way he sees it and partake in the joy that he has when he looks at his creation. According to German psychologist Michael Titze, children laugh over 100 times a day, whereas adults only laugh about 15 times. I wonder if this is another reason why Jesus said we need to approach the kingdom of God like children, ready to see and take part in the joy. Sometimes boys can be nervous of expressing this joy: it may not be cool, or they might have a sense of church being a very serious business. Without turning into hysterical hyenas, we need to be prepared to laugh more. As you are more joyful, so your boys will be more joyful.

Boundaries

Children can use humour as a weapon of choice, so it needs to be clear where the boundaries are. It is not acceptable to say cruel things or hurtful things about other people, even if they are funny. Equally, however, we need to allow boys to play with humour, and not shut down toilet humour too soon. They need to know what is acceptable and not acceptable, and where different types of conversation may or may not be appropriate.

Things to think about

- What makes you laugh? When was the last time you had a really good laugh?
- When was the last time your team or family laughed together?
- What do you need to do to reignite and sustain your joy?
- Where are your humour boundaries? Do they need adjusting?

6. ROCK AND PAPER AND SCISSORS
MUSIC AND CREATIVITY

'Boys don't do crafts.' The words were echoing down the length of the damp marquee in the evening gloom. They had been said at the team briefing the day before when the activities for the week had been explained; and now, 150 children and many long, wet hours later, they seemed to have taken on a greater significance. And yet there on the 'drying table' was the evidence. Row after row of paper plates filled with clay creations ranging from what looked like a pile of peas to something resembling the Leaning Tower of Pisa – some of which had been made by girls and some by boys. Sometimes it was obvious who had made what, but what was more obvious was that all of them had got something out of this activity, and their creativity proved it.

If children do not separate the sacred and the secular, as has already been suggested, then we need to offer them an 'integrated' approach to connecting with God. Our biblical teaching should flow through every activity, explicitly and implicitly. This means that a programme that offers the key teaching themes through a variety of activities including music and creative arts will feel natural to the children, and can help them 'understand' the content at a number of different levels.

What is important, though, is that we do not limit the children's sensual experience to the five physical senses, but also allow them to experience what has been described as the myriad of 'abstract senses'[1] which enable them to engage with and interpret the world around them. It is my belief that our Western world-view has trapped us into thinking in terms of linear development, with developmental stages being checked from birth, through SATs, to A-level exams and beyond, and that this contributes to the separating of senses. When children decide they do not like curry because it is 'too minty' or 'too breathy', we correct them and tell them that it is 'too hot or spicy', or when they tell us about the colours of music, perhaps we tell them not to be silly, shutting down their attempts to describe the sensations. Instead we should be prepared not to rationalize our experiences too quickly, and allow our children to re-teach us how to really see, hear and feel. Equally, if we do not rate our own artistic or musical abilities (or theirs!) we are too ready not to see it as spiritual. I have dozens of pictures of me, by various children, that look absolutely nothing like me (I hope!), but to those children they represent value, connection and relationship way beyond the cost of the materials or even the time.

The arts and creativity

The Eastern theological tradition has a long history of using visual art to aid spiritual transformation, believing that beauty in this world orientates us towards God, who is the foundation and epitome of beautiful things.[2] In the West, Protestantism has caused us to shy away a little from this celebration of artistic beauty, and although many of our churches are still beautiful places, they often lack the richness of colour and symbolism that can be found elsewhere in the world.

Children like beautiful things, or at least things that represent beauty to them, and many of the boys in my research identified inspirational pictures as a helpful spiritual connection and a way to think about their connection with God. From about two years on, children become more and more able to master various cultural symbols,[3] and can use this ability to interpret art for themselves. They can also be prolific producers of art, and again can use this medium to interpret and express feelings and understandings. Many of the world's most famous painters are men, and they did not all discover their ability as adults!

'Making things and being creative' was important to the boys who attended X:site and the children's church. Much of that interest, however, is dependent on what the craft is and whether the boys see a purpose to it. There also has to be a realization that just because the boys are engaging with it, it does not always make it a spiritual activity. One of the boys in a children's church focus group was honest enough to admit, 'I just get thinking about what I am making more than why I am making it.'

Statistically, 'looking at pictures' was a popular activity. What was particularly interesting, though, was how the boys in the RE lessons engaged with the pictures. I divided the classes into small groups and gave each group one of a selection of 'fine art' pictures to look at.[4] I then asked them to do some detective work and discover the symbols of the Christian faith that they could find in the picture, and I also asked what they thought the artist was trying to convey with colours, technique and so on. It worked really well, and I was amazed at some of the things that the boys pointed out, not just in terms of the symbols but also about how the colours and painting made them feel.

Drama

Tony Eaude believes that drama, another creative art, is a particularly important activity for boys, who perhaps struggle to pick up the skills required to express empathy and relationship.[5] By experimenting within someone else's stories, boys can practise the skills needed to interpret their own story or those of their friends. Drama was a popular activity amongst the boys in children's church. Interestingly, at the X:sites 'acting' was less popular with the boys than with the girls, but there were large variances across the events, indicating again that whether the boys find this engaging is probably more about the ability of those leading the session and how the activity is introduced and modelled by leaders (particularly men). It could also be to do with peer pressure. If boys are constructing their masculinity in *opposition* to femininity, then if an activity is perceived to be 'feminine', the boys may automatically dissociate themselves from it.

Music

Music has been used as a means of spiritual connection since before Christendom, although the church also has a long history of music, and much of what we call 'classical music' today has been influenced by the Christian tradition. As many children spontaneously sing and make music, and many adolescents treat music as an alternative religion,[6] it seems clear that music can communicate in a way that we do not understand and can therefore offer the child a means of experiencing something beyond the 'normal'.

'Singing and music' were the most popular ways to hear from God, with about a third of both the girls and boys expressing a preference. Although it got a mixed reaction from the children's church members, there is enough evidence to indicate just how important music is as a spiritual connection, whether this is worship music or other musical activity. Trish Graves believes that if age-appropriate songs are used or meanings are explained, then children will be able to focus on God and discover more about him.[7] I think this is true, but also believe that we do not need to limit the spirituality of music to Christian music. Watching the televised 'Help for Heroes' concert recently, I was intrigued by the sense of spirituality present as the audience spontaneously sang Robbie Williams's song 'Angels'. Bound together by the common currency of the words, and by the emotion and excitement of the event, this was a community working together to create something beautiful and meaningful to them.

Throughout the Bible, worship is carried out in many different ways and the styles of worship God ordained for the people of Israel used all the senses. The posture for worship was sometimes kneeling,[8] or even prostration,[9] but standing (often with uplifted hands) was a common attitude for prayer in Jewish worship,[10] and it is probable that early Christians also adopted it. A model of spiritual formation that offers boys a multisensory and physically interactive opportunity for worship will not only engage those with different learning styles, but will also allow them to respond with their whole body, giving physical expression to the thoughts and feelings that they are holding inside. Many children chose 'dancing and jumping about' as a preferred way to respond to God, which perhaps reflects the physicality of their emotional and spiritual response and means that we should not ignore the potential these two activities have for helping boys connect with God.

 So how . . . do we encourage boys to engage with and express their spirituality through the arts, creativity and music?

Creative charisma

What is important is that we do not confine our understanding of creativity to painting and drawing, art forms which many boys consider themselves poor at and therefore constrained in, and that other opportunities for creative expression are offered, like sculpture, drama and percussion. Cooking offers a whole wealth of creative possibilities that can be a multi-sensory experience. What is also key, if boys are to get the most out of an activity and be able to use it to express their spirituality and connect with God, is that they have leaders who are passionate about what they are doing. If you do not feel that you are creative or dramatic, bring in someone who is for that part of your programme. Or get together with a couple of other families and share the gifts and passions that you have that can inspire your boys.

Construction and creativity

Boys *do* do craft, but the type of craft and what it is called needs to be chosen carefully. Perhaps surprisingly, Hama beads work very well, as does clay.

Some research has suggested that women have stronger aesthetic interests than men, who have a greater interest in technology.[11] This may explain why Lego and Meccano will occupy some boys for hours on end, and I believe that this expression of their creativity could also be a time when their mind and spirit can wander and 'connect'. Be prepared to give boys the time to engage in the activity. Recently at our Friday night club, we had a variety of activities on offer, including clay. One boy kept going back to the clay table to make something else. During the course of the evening, as he made little clay figures to represent the leaders and his friends, we discovered all sorts of things about what we meant to him and how he felt he related to people in the group.

Make it big

One of the reasons why boys get frustrated with 'craft activities' is that many of them still have not quite mastered the fine motor skills that are required to make something that looks as they want it to look. Take out the stress, and make whatever it is on a larger scale. Use big paper and decorating paintbrushes to create a picture, flip-pad paper to create an origami frog, packing boxes to make a Goliath. Or how about making a large-scale picture of the Bible story together using household items like they do on *Art Attack* and *SMart*?

Digitalize

Digital technology means that you can give your boys the opportunities to engage with their spirituality through photography and graphic art, at very little cost. They can animate a song that means something to them, or take pictures of places or things that fill them with awe. Microphotography can increase the sense of wonder, as they explore the unseen patterns that make up our world.

Picture it!

Use pictures wherever possible. Fine art, cartoons, whatever – boys find looking at something helpful in connecting with their spirituality, so give them something to look at, not just as part of your story or activity but as permanent features in your meeting rooms. You might find the Brick Testament helpful as the pictures show Bible stories depicted by Lego characters.[12] Make sure you check them through properly, though. I got caught out when I thought the story of Joseph might entertain my daughter after her appendicitis operation. It did, as the first few pictures were of Jacob 'begetting' all twelve of his sons, with a huge painted grin on his little Lego face!

Praying in colour

Take a roll of wallpaper, some paint and some decorating paintbrushes. Explain that they are going to pray in colour – they do not have to create pictures, they do not have to write words, they are just going to use the colours to help them focus their thoughts and express their prayers. Alternatively, if you have the resources, use coloured lights to convey different prayer moods and modes.

Rockin'

The most popular way to hear from God, with about a third of both the girls and boys expressing a preference, was through 'singing and music'. I imagine that for some this is maybe through their own musical activity, but for many this is probably an expression of the connection with God they experience when they join in singing at church and at events like X:site. Boys do sing, particularly if they are confident of the words and the tune, but will find it difficult if they feel exposed – if, for instance, your group is quite small, or new songs are constantly being introduced. My observations at X:site 6 identified that the boys were just as engaged as the girls through most of the songs. However, with songs that had complicated, more choreographed and dance-like actions, less confident boys would soon disengage. All the boys were fully engaged for songs which involved actions that meant that they could jump on, lean on or touch each other. The simplest form of physical engagement with a song is 'air guitar', so encourage the boys to 'rock out' as they worship. If this is not appropriate, perhaps in a school assembly or quiet worship service, then make sure the words are easy to read (for younger boys read them through to them before you start singing) and the tune simple to pick up.

Things to think about

- Are you creative? If not, who can you get on board to help you with this part of your activities?
- Do you offer a wide enough range of creative activities?
- What is the environment like in which your boys are living/working/worshipping? Do you need to do something radical to make it more inspirational?

7. PAUSES AND PONDERINGS
THINKING

When I am all alone envy me most,
Then my thoughts flutter round me in a glimmering host;
Some dressed in silver, some dressed in white,
Each like a taper blossoming light[1]

Some writers on childhood have suggested that boys do not perform as well as girls in tasks like reading, talking about feelings and quiet introspection because a part of the brain called the *corpus callosum* is smaller in boys than in girls. I am not, however, convinced, as although the scientific research did find differences between men and women in the size of this part of the brain, those who carried it out did not feel that these differences were significant in children aged between two and sixteen.[2] Instead I think we have to look at other significant variables, including the nature of the sex chromosomes and sex hormones and, more importantly, behavioural and cultural effects that influence the development and performance of girls versus boys. Small differences which may be physically present are accentuated by the opportunities and encouragements that the children receive as they develop, which explains why some boys perfect their fine motor skills and introspective tendencies by spending hours alone playing with Lego, and some girls with huge vocabularies still cannot catch a ball in Year 6.

I would argue that there is still a tendency to think of boys only in terms of activity, noise and physicality – a belief that if we send them out to play football, all will be well. But this belief not only does a disservice to those quieter boys who watch from the sidelines, think deeply and often confound us with the depth of their questioning and understanding; it also does a disservice to those boys who are active, intimating that they are only one-dimensional and are incapable of engaging emotionally and spiritually in any other way.

Silence

If you walk down any high street in England, at any time of day, you will see someone talking on their phone, and if you cannot see their hand lifted to their ear, then you might suspect they are talking to themselves (or, even more embarrassingly, to you) until you spot their hands-free kit. I wonder if the reason why the mobile phone and social networks have become so successful is because, in talking or being available to talk, people can prove to themselves that they are not lonely. Our deepest desire is to love and be loved, and our phonebook, or Facebook friends list, proves that we are loved. Or does it? Do the constant noise, distraction and status updates instead mask what we are afraid to face: a deeper fear of ourselves and our inadequacies? We tend to think of 'silence' in negative terms, evoking images of exam halls and dusty old libraries, but if we describe it in terms of space, calm, peace, hush and stillness, immediately we can see the spiritual and healing qualities that it can represent. When was the last time you sat in complete silence? Now think of the children you work with. How many minutes in a day do you think they spend without noise, most of it generated electronically?

The ability to be still and silent is within all of us, but just like most other areas of our life, it needs to be exercised like a muscle. You cannot expect a boy who has been brought up on a diet of junk food to convert to, and relish, bowls of brown rice straight away. Neither can you expect boys who have been submerged in a perpetual barrage of noise and visual stimulation to sit still and meditate for hours on end. But if we do not help them to exercise this muscle, then not only will we bruise their spirituality now, but we may also set them up for a long-term spiritual disability. Apparently, most people say that their spiritual awareness occurs most often when they are alone.[3] Is it not therefore important for our boys to find themselves alone and quiet every now and then?

Some would argue that for active boys, sitting and listening, thinking and wondering is boring, and will not engage their attention long enough to be meaningful. Scottie May, a leading thinker on contemplative children's spirituality in the States, disputes this by saying that these people have mis-understood children, and are acting on what children say they want rather than carefully observing what they actually long for.[4] Silence has been described as a 'universal need',[5] but I think it is a need that requires some specific opportunity and support in order to be met. If boys are not given space and stillness to be, to breathe, to focus on their body and their surroundings, to wonder and ponder, then I really believe they will be like the hard, dried-up path in Jesus' parable of the sower. Equally, if children have never been given the opportunity, or the wherewithal, to experience silence and face the fear of themselves and their own inadequacies while still in infancy, they will find it so much harder when they reach adulthood.

Thinking and philosophizing

Spiritual connections include activities such as thinking and philosophizing, and experiencing mystery and wonder. These go beyond the simple transmission of biblical information to offer the opportunity to encounter God in ways that engender a sense of awe, a heightened awareness and an unfrightened bewilderment that is able to hold complexities in tension without being overwhelmed. These connections, although not necessarily popular across the board, are important for some children, particularly boys. In one of the children's church focus groups, one boy commented that he did not believe that thinking and wondering on his own was a spiritual connection, but then he described in great detail how he used time on his own to process his day and make sense and meaning. Some children are unaware that this is an important part of their life. In the RE lessons, it was clear that activities which encouraged the children to think about what they had seen or heard and relate it to something else were effective. What was difficult to ascertain was how effective these activities were in enhancing spiritual development.

It has been said that the drive for meaning is as acute as the drive for physical survival,[6] which is why for many boys 'thinking' is an important part of their lives, and Pooh Bear is described as putting time aside for 'Grand Thoughts'. Children ask a lot of questions and sometimes it feels that the answers we give drop into a bottomless pool. As we encourage boys to ask questions and ponder things, we have to be careful that we do not give them all the answers. Boys who love *Scooby Doo* will tell you that the worst bit about it is that you know that the first person the gang meet is going to be the one in the costume at the end! If we clear up the mystery by nailing down all the answers, we destroy it. Jesus very rarely explained any of his parables, and often answered questions with questions, thereby allowing us to 'own' our understanding as we work things out for ourselves.

Here is where we meet the fulcrum of the balancing scales of spirituality on the one side, and Christian faith development on the other. Too often we have been so desperate to 'save and disciple' children that we have filled their heads with theological and biblical facts. In doing so we have sometimes been in danger of destroying that fragile dragonfly of their spirituality. But just as Jesus grew in knowledge and wisdom,[7] so our children need to know the content of our faith in order to grow in it.

The Bible is a fundamental part of what Christians believe is our communication from God, but, as the Emerging Church writer Brian McLaren points out, it is 'an extremely difficult book for modern and postmodern readers alike'.[8] It has long been believed that systematic and thorough teaching and memorization should overcome this hurdle. The God-given instruction to teach the Word of God to our children[9] became a motive for education in the Judaistic culture[10] that was inherited by early Christians. In fact, church history shows that whenever missionaries planted churches, they almost always planted schools.[11] Learning, however, is not just about being able to repeat by rote. There are lots of ways in which we can make the content of our faith and our Bible interesting to learn and memorable. What we have to avoid, though, is making the information inert – learned but not necessarily understood in a way that changes behaviour. Many years ago a brother and sister were part of my Sunday morning group. He knew so much information about the Bible, it was astounding. He left his sister standing when it came to reciting the books of the Bible, the names of the disciples, the places that Paul visited, and so on. At the time I was very concerned that he had a great deal of head knowledge, but no heart knowledge. Unfortunately, he has proved me right in that, unlike his sister, as an adult he appears to have little or no faith.

Many of our boys love facts. They collect facts about dinosaurs, cars, sports teams, and so on. Wouldn't it be good if they collected facts about God's story? Yes, but . . . Neurologists have given us insights into the role of the mid-brain in emotional processing, describing how emotional processing needs more time and space than cognitive processes. If, as children's workers, we want to facilitate spiritual development and, as Christians, we want to encourage boys in relationship with Jesus, then we need to avoid giving those boys too much inert information, or not enough time to process what they have seen or experienced.

There is also the additional problem that for many boys academic and intellectual work has been feminized. In some state schools, boys who are seen to work too hard may be teased,[12] and therefore many of them, in their attempts to find their masculine identity, may well shy away from a model of ministry that is based around a 'big book' and awards intellectual prowess. One possible way of overcoming this, however, is to give children the opportunity to meet in single-sex groups, thereby giving the boys the opportunity to explore a more cognitive framework for their spirituality without the fear of comparison with the 'wrong' gender.

Ritual

Anyone who has had to read the same bedtime story over and over again will be familiar with the concept that children are fascinated by, and content with, repetition. Rituals can make children feel secure as they offer a familiar framework and stability, and for boys this can be particularly pertinent. Indeed, in other cultures, much is made of the 'coming of age' and many traditions hold rituals of initiation for boys, as a means of giving order to individual and community activity. In many African tribes, traditionally boys become men after a lengthy preparation and the ritual of circumcision. In the Hindu and Jewish faith traditions, there are also significant sacred ceremonies for boys.

According to Biddulph, boys feel insecure if there is not enough structure in the situation in which they find themselves; he argues that their testosterone-driven make-up leads them to want to establish a pecking order and create hierarchies, which is harder to do when they are all the same age.[13] He believes that if we create the structure then they can relax; they can stop covering up their fear by 'acting tough' and get on with the activities they want to do. Hans Asperger contends that the reason why boys appear to have a higher rate of diagnosis for Asperger's syndrome and autism is because they are at the extreme end of a spectrum of behaviours normally associated with 'maleness' which include things like attention to detail and single-minded focus.[14] Often 'we know more than we can tell', with much of our knowing remaining inaccessible to our consciousness and our ability to verbalize it.[15] This may be particularly so for children who do not yet have a full range of vocabulary or experience to compare and contrast with, and who perhaps need longer to access this 'knowledge' and interpret it. For boys, then, it would appear that Sunday school or after-school club programmes which use ritual and repetition and are detailed in their storytelling may actually be more engaging and better equipped to help them develop spiritually and connect with God.

We do have to be careful, however, that the ritual that gives structure does not become a burden that stifles creativity and lacks integrity when it does not match the real-life experiences of the participants. Churches are places where many rituals, simple and complex, are conducted, but Barley sounds a salutary note when she says that much church worship could be in danger of becoming 'pure entertainment and at times even emotional self-fulfilment when what people are often seeking is quiet, prayerful spirituality and a sense of mystery'.[16]

Prayer

Prayer still remains one of the most popular 'spiritual connections', despite the apparent secularization of our culture.[17] In 1967 some American psychologists looked at the subject of children and prayer.[18] They discovered that between the ages of ten and twelve, children's prayers tended to be formulaic and consisted mainly of requests to their god. However, as they moved into adolescence, the prayers were more likely to take the form of a private conversation. In an article on prayer in *The Times*, one author suggests that children are capable of praying for one minute for every year of their life.[19] It was unclear from the article whether that ratio differs between boys and girls. This is a shame, because prayer was the single spiritual connection where there seemed to be the most significant difference between the responses from the girls who attended the X:site events, and those from the boys, who indicated a strong preference for 'praying quietly on my own'.

This was also reflected in the responses to the 'I feel . . . ' posters, and in the discussions at the Anglican children's church, where two groups of boys placed 'praying quietly on my own' high up in their ranking, and in one group there was quite an extended conversation about how the boys prayed quietly on their own and what they prayed about. This need for time alone is corroborated by other evidence, including research which suggests that, compared to women, twice as many men were converted when they were on their own, and indicates spiritual activity done in private rather than in public.[20]

When I shared these findings with one mother, she burst into tears in front of me. I was slightly worried that I had said something to offend her deeply, but instead they were tears of relief. She had been worrying that every time she had tried to pray with her son at bedtime, he had not seemed that inter-ested. I have video footage of him telling me all about his prayer life. It was not that he did not want to pray, he just wanted to do it in private. Now there is a danger here, that we absolve ourselves of all responsibility of praying with our boys, believing that they are doing it for themselves. Of course, we need to continue to include them in public prayer and corporate worship as well as equip them and encourage them in their private prayer life. Not just because it is important that they feel they belong to a worshipping community, but also because there is evidence to suggest that it may actually have a significant impact on their long-term health and well-being.[21]

 So how . . . do we encourage boys to engage with and express their spirituality through silence, ritual, thinking and philosophizing and prayer?

Exercise your own silence muscle

Many of us might feel uncomfortable in trying to teach boys techniques that can help them in silent reflection, for the sole reason that we are not very good at it ourselves. If your silence and stillness 'muscle' is a bit creaky from lack of use, try to carve out little pockets of time in which you can exercise it and focus on being, and on waiting on God.[22] They do not necessarily have to be specific times or places, or even always intentional. When you are forced to wait for something or someone, use that time constructively. One evening a couple of years ago, I had a meeting arranged with the vicar, but when I arrived at the church he was busy talking to someone else. I sat down to wait, frustrated by the inactivity and 'waste' of time. I cannot remember what prompted me, but I decided to use the time to rest in God's presence. I slowed down my breathing and waited, turning my heart and mind to patience rather than frustration. As I waited, I felt God's presence descend on me, not heavily, but like summer rain on my face. It was the most amazing experience and just what I needed. Now, when I feel myself getting stressed, I know it is time to sit and wait, and turn my face to the sky.

Exercise the children's silence muscle

As a result of the discovery of the importance of silence, we have tried to intersperse our activities in children's church with silent episodes. For instance, as part of a 'travelling story' about Jacob, we rested at 'Bethel', to see if God wanted to say something to us, like he had to Jacob. We told the children to lie down and relax, and listen to God. Initially this kind of activity was greeted with a certain amount of fidgeting, par-ticularly from the boys, but with some gentle encouragements to lie still, and even the odd bit of head-stroking, we reached a place where it was clear that all the children were still and settled and that those who wanted to had an opportunity to connect with God in this way.

Having a candle lit for the children to gather round as they come in, or getting them to focus on their breathing before you tell a story are other ways of helping them to find the space in which to exercise their spirituality in quietness.

Revamp your rituals

There are many parts of your time together with your boys that already hold elements of routine and ritual. It may be the type of biscuits that you always buy; it may be the greeting, or programme, that has pattern and repetition. Of course there is a danger of getting stuck in a rut and becoming frightened of change, but watch the boys themselves for where they see the rituals that make them feel secure and where their feelings of insecurity could be reduced by the introduction of a ritual.

Rituals are not just about routine, they are also meant to signify importance and demonstrate rites of passage. Think about what rites of passage your church family provides for the children as they grow from infancy to adulthood, and what rituals you have to help your boys make the transition to men.

At home, use events in the church calendar to add structure to your boys' year. As my children have got older and busier, we have struggled to do the daily Advent Bible reading that we used to do when they were little. Now we use Nativity characters once or twice a week to help us think about the Christmas story and what Advent means as we build the scene during December.

Private prayer tools

If boys are praying quietly on their own, then we need to help them to do this in a way that grows with them and sustains them. For younger boys, one possibility is helping them to collect a set of pictures of the people they love, or the things they are concerned about, which they can stick to their wall to create a prayer focus. Or they can make prayer beads with different colours representing different things that they would like to talk to God about. For older boys it might be worth doing some simple Ignatian-style exercises together, to equip them with a format to use on their own. For instance, below is a version of the five-step 'Daily Examen' that St Ignatius practised.[23]

1. Become aware of God's presence.
2. Review the day with gratitude.
3. Pay attention to your emotions.
4. Choose one feature of the day and pray from it.
5. Look toward tomorrow.

Perpetuate the ponder

Many boys will not answer a question if they think it has a right or wrong answer and they do not know what the right one is. 'Wondering' with them helps them to see that it is not necessary to have it all sewn up and understood before they join in the discussion. Allow the children to play with their ideas and even the biblical text, in the same way that they might play with a ball. Some of them might want to roll it backwards and forwards, watching the pattern move; others may want to throw it as high as possible and see where it lands; still others might want to enjoy passing it to their friends and waiting for them to pass it back. We also need to give our boys time to process the things that they have heard, and then an opportunity to come back to us with their thoughts. When planning a programme, consider where the 'pauses' are in your activities which give the boys an opportunity to do nothing, or perhaps to use their hands while they let their minds wander and wonder.

As a parent, you can help your boys to ponder by asking questions that begin with the phrase 'I wonder' or 'What if', or by turning off the television and the radio, lighting a candle and snuggling up for some time to breathe and watch it burn, and to think and ponder.

Things to think about

- Which boys in your group will be relieved by the opportunity to practise stillness and silence? Which boys might struggle?
- Are your activities developing the children's 'head knowledge' or 'heart knowledge'? Do you need to change things to redress the balance?
- Are you or your team ready to allow the children to 'play' with ideas and not dish out the answers? If not, what can you do to be ready?

8. THE ELEVENTH COMMANDMENT
SERVICE

The cars whooshed by as the Sunday lunchtime traffic got under-way, the sun was beating down on the back of our necks, and I thought I might never stand up properly again. Myself and half a dozen eleven- to fourteen-year-old lads were weeding the paved area outside the church and church hall. It was a beautiful, hot, sunny day, and none of us had really wanted to stay inside and use our brains in children's church, so we had come up with this half-baked idea to pull up the abundant weeds that had sprouted between the paving stones. Only it was not half-baked – hot and uncomfortable work, yes, but the boys really loved it, and most of them did not stop until it was done. While we bent and scraped, sometimes in companionable silence, we also talked and laughed, and the boys developed a narrative about what they were doing and why it was important to themselves and as a gift to the congregation.

While a model of spiritual engagement that encourages contemplation, thinking and wondering may give boys the opportunity to think about their spirituality, I am not convinced that it gives them the chance to act on it. Buechner suggests that 'to worship God means to serve him' and that there are two ways of doing this: 'doing things for him that you need to do' and 'doing things for him that he needs to have done'.[1] As I mentioned in the opening chapter (see p. 21), Gutiérrez argues that spirituality is about living out our relationship with God in community.[2] Watching and listening over the years, I have become aware that for many boys there is an eleventh commandment – to look after the planet on which they live. And so in this chapter I want to explore not just the significance of nature for boys' connections with God, but also the relevance of acts of service or 'good works' in their expression of their spirituality.

Nature as a playground

I have a favourite place in the Derbyshire hills where I can stare out over fields, woods, villages and farms, into a seemingly endless horizon. It is a place where I can feel deeply, physically, emotionally and spiritually; where the almighty vista fills me with awe, and the wind can whip away my cries of joy and pain; where I can watch the miniature action of animals and people below me with hope, disillusionment and contentment. For many of us, solitude and 'silence' can be found in the great outdoors, and therefore 'nature' seems to me to be an obvious 'spiritual connection', closely allied to 'the arts', which reflects the importance of beauty, and to 'wonder and mystery', which reflects the complexity of the natural world. The Celtic Christian spirituality has a strong tradition of God in nature, and many tribal people share with ancient Israel the theological understanding of the intimate relationship between people and land. None of the models of spirituality I looked at mention nature as a means for children to connect with their spirituality, despite Hart's belief that 'nature seems to resonate deeply within us' and is 'the most common trigger for ecstasy'.[3] For the children who attended the X:site events, it did appear to have some impact, particularly for the boys, and it was a recurring theme in the discussions with the boys in the children's church, and in the RE lessons.

In his discussion on creation in *Through the Eyes of a Child*, Keith White uses an excerpt from the writings of Choan-Seng Song to illustrate how important nature might be in children's theological reflection as a vehicle for listening and observing; and he goes on to suggest that their active engagement with nature is something we can learn from.[4] He also reminds us again of the importance of play, and describes one little boy's reaction to the 'great big adventure playground' that is Snowdonia. Just as the psalmist was inspired to worship God by what he could see, our responsibility therefore is to offer boys as many opportunities as possible to engage with this 'adventure playground' and to marvel at and be inspired by it.

A world without beauty can, I believe, stifle a child's spirituality, although thankfully it has been observed that children will find things to inspire fascination and wonder in the ugliest of places.[5] I do not believe that this gives us permission to surround them with ugliness, but rather it allows us to wonder at their capacity to delight despite it, and offers us a remit to provide all our children with opportunities to be surrounded by beauty. Looking at God's creation or at pictures of it was the second most preferred way to hear from God amongst the boys at X:site, and so we need to give them lots of things to look at.

Actions speak louder?

Some would suggest that the outward activity of the child is a sign of an inward process. Indeed, in his helpful book for teachers on spiritual development, David Smith says that 'the difference between spiritual growth and its absence becomes visible in actions'.[6] Other writers say that the heightened sense of 'connectedness' that is characteristic of spirituality will inevitably lead to a passion for justice and action.[7] As many children are kinaesthetic learners, in that they learn by doing, it may well be that by doing something for someone else in service, a child will experience that connectedness in a way that is real to them. The danger of suggesting that for some children 'good works' may be a spiritual connection is that we are standing on the precipice of a 'faith by works' view of spirituality. It is therefore important that instead we concentrate on a holistic view of spirituality that includes contemplation *and* action.

Kohlberg's theory of moral development suggests that up until the age of about ten, children are in stages one and two of pre-conventional morality.[8] At stage one, punishment 'proves' that disobedience is wrong. At stage two, punishment is a risk that one naturally wants to avoid. On the 'I feel . . .' posters there were many responses that related to 'doing something right or good'. My question, as I reviewed the research data, and one that I think we need to ask for ourselves about our boys, was this: does the 'doing something right' come from a response to God's love, or from a sense that it will reap a right reward, or, perhaps more worryingly, because they do not feel accepted when they do not do something right or whatever is perceived to be 'good'? In this project there was no mechanism to test to what extent the spiritual development experienced by the children had impacted their morality. It was interesting, however, to witness the expressions of morality made by the children in the RE lessons. Watson argues that spirituality is about 'enabling the creative thinking and relational feeling necessary for the development of morality and a sense of community'.[9] In this case, perhaps these 'moral' statements could be taken as an indication of spirituality.

For many children, as the graph on the next page shows, helping other people and looking after God's creation are significant ways of expressing their response to him and their spirituality.

With the exception of one event, both these active expressions of connection with others and the world were generally popular amongst all the children, but especially the boys. Both of these responses also featured highly in the discussions at the children's church. I believe 'looking after God's creation' may be higher because of the discussion of environmental issues at school, but also because of the link with pets. Many boys get a great deal of joy and solace out of looking after or just being with an animal. For many years my parents ran camps for primary-aged children, and for four weeks every summer our entire household, including our dog Gandalph, would live in a field with hundreds of children. Not only was Gandalph a useful alarm if strangers came onto the site, but he was also a good friend to those children – and in particular the boys – who felt a bit homesick or needed some space.

It is intriguing how the response to 'helping others' varies so greatly across the different X:sites. Once again this indicates the importance of the attitudes of the leaders present, but I also wonder whether 'helping others' was not chosen as an option by more children because many of them are still not encouraged to take active roles in things. It has been argued that the litmus test of genuine spirituality is the extent to which it cultivates a sense of responsibility for others,[10] so high results

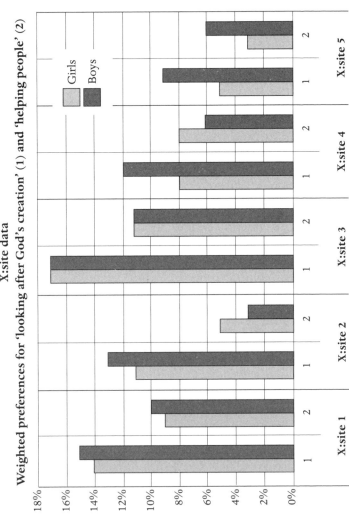

X:site data

Weighted preferences for 'looking after God's creation' (1) and 'helping people' (2) for this element could indicate a greater level of spiritual awareness than you might find with a different group of children. If we are to encourage boys to take a greater responsibility for others around them, then perhaps this will make them more spiritually aware and improve their connections with God as they work through why this is important and how it makes them feel.

 So how . . . do we encourage boys to engage with and express their spirituality through nature and 'good works'?

Look, see

Get your boys outside as much as possible to see the wonders of creation around them. Even in a concrete jungle there are pockets of greenery that you can explore; weeds might not be appreciated by gardeners, but they can teach us a lot about resilience and optimism! If you cannot find greenery, then lie on your backs and look at the wonder of the sky. Use water and sand as ways of connecting with the physical sensations of being part of creation. What does it feel like to have the wind in his hair (even if it is only the wind in an underground tube tunnel)? What effect do the different types of light (seasonal and daily variations) have on how he thinks and feels about things? How do the vastness of a tree and the minuteness of veins on a leaf help him to understand his place in the world?

'Church on the Hill'

One Sunday a couple of years ago, nobody in our family wanted to go to church. I tried to explain how it was important that we met with the people of God, but I was not even convincing myself! Instead we decided to do what we have since labelled 'Church on the Hill'. We made some hot chocolate, bundled into the car and drove up to our nearest hill, singing worship choruses on the way. On the hill we chased the dog, climbed trees and played hide and seek. Then we sat on a blanket and read a Bible story as we drank the hot chocolate. Gazing out over the countryside, we talked about what it might mean for us, before we prayed about the week to come. Beautiful surroundings and play, Bible and prayer, can be an intoxicating combination, and for boys who are militating against 'boring' Sunday school classes, this might be a simple but effective way of re-engaging them.

Sacred Salvage Service

As mentioned before, children are better at not separating the sacred and the secular than adults. For many boys, looking after their planet is an expression of how they feel about their connection with it, their Creator and their fellow human beings. Some may have done conservation projects at school, some may even have taken part in a 'Wastewatchers' week.[11] Why not get your boys involved in doing a recycling and fair-trade audit of your church, club or group? What resources are you wasting? What can be recycled? What could be bought fair-trade instead? As they identify the opportunities, they can also volunteer to take responsibility for that particular area or activity. It might seem like a small thing, but for some boys, being in charge of taking home the plastic bottles at the end of club time to put in their recycling box may be a really important way of not just expressing their care of the environment, but also allowing them to serve the community and helping them to feel they belong to it.

Doing a Dorcas

It is not just saving the planet that is important to children. Many of them are really passionate about serving others in little and big ways. About once a term we try to have a charity night, when the children bake cakes to raise money for something, or write or draw pictures about a particular issue which then get sent off to their local MP. But it does not have to be for those in need. Many of the boys I have worked with seem to get a real sense of worth and value from helping set up and clear away the activities. This summer we introduced another new workshop at a Scripture Union Mission. We called it 'Doing a Dorcas', based on the story from Acts of Dorcas, who served her community by making them clothes. It involved the children (mainly boys) in volunteering to help with small jobs like weeding and chair-moving around the school where we were meeting.

Something to care for

One of the things that struck me during the series of RE lessons was how often the topic of animals came up in conversation. I wonder if for children there is a deeper spiritual significance to animals than perhaps we realize as adults. You will probably not be very popular if you suggest to the parents of all the boys in your group that they need a dog to enhance their spirituality! But are there other ways in which you can give the children an opportunity to experience awe and wonder at the complexity of God's creation, and the sense of purpose and reward that comes from the responsibility of caring for something else? One way that might not be as costly as a trip to the zoo or getting a group hamster is creating a small vegetable garden. You would not believe the pride that my son has just shown as he paraded one of his parsnips that is now actually big enough to eat!

Beautify the background

The National Advisory Committee on Creative and Cultural Education argues that people need to be supported by environments that do not stifle creativity but allow learning that is creative and cross-context.[12] My experience is that children's church often gets the smallest, dullest, least popular space available. While the children's environment *per se* is not, I believe, a spiritual connection, I do think it has an impact on their ability to make connections through other means – and an environment that gives them stimulus and space, and the opportunity to experiment and be still, will go a long way towards providing them with the opportunities to engage with their spirituality that are lacking in many of our churches.

Things to think about

- What male role models are there who serve in your church? Could they mentor some of your boys as they serve others?
- In what ways can your boys communicate their passion about nature and service to the rest of the congregation?
- In what ways are you personally modelling service and stewardship?

9. THRILLS AND SPILLS
RISK

The group of young teenage lads was from a broken Midlands town, their eyes sharp and aggressive as they hid deep in dirty hoodies. The journey from their world of rusting industrial estates and shabby retail parks into the Welsh mountains was lost to harsh voices, swearing and sexual insults between bouts of violence.

That evening they got back on the minibus flushed with excitement, hoodies pulled back to show smiles and sparkling eyes as they retold each other of their mountain adventures. With soft voices they reassured each other how they'd been scared but still done it. The swearing lessened and the fights stopped, in their own difficult words they told how the fear, adventure and achievement had taken them outside of what they thought they were, how they had glimpsed more about who they really are.[1]

Speed, height, noise, space, action all serve to fill a little boy's body with adrenaline and excite his senses. Children engage in risky behaviour for a number of reasons, not least to get our attention! But for many children, particularly boys, risk-taking is one of the few ways in which they can regain some influence or control in their world and try to experience a sense of 'other' not experienced elsewhere in their lives. I am not suggesting that we should be encouraging boys to play on railway lines, or young men to drive fast with no lights in the dark, just so that they can have a 'spiritual experience', but rather that we should consider the idea that for some boys, exciting stimulus and the adrenaline rush of taking a risk may be important.

Although we should not forget the children in this country who are not protected, neither must we forget that many children in the UK are overprotected when it comes to the little losses of life. This means that their 'coping muscles' are too weak when something big happens and therefore, instead of resilient children who bend with and grow through loss and transition, we are increasingly seeing brittle children who break at the first big blow. Fear can be a constructive emotion, helping us to work out what to pay attention to and to learn where the real dangers are and how to overcome them. Unhealthy fear, on the other hand, can be constricting and debilitating.

Over forty years ago, people writing about children were expressing concern about the 'negative dread' that was filling our society and suggesting that children do actually need to experience 'healthy fear' in order to utilize the positive force that it can unleash in terms of creativity, thought and enquiry.[2] The 'culture of fear' has got worse, despite the fact that statistically speaking children are safer now than at any point in history, and as a result children's freedom to experience reality has been severely curtailed. Some go as far as to say that for some children their childhood looks more like a prison sentence lived out behind locked doors.[3] It is important, then, that our desire to keep children safe does not drive out the opportunities they should have for experiment and development, and does not make their world so 'safe' that they are not free to be creative and grow.

I believe that 'risk' is an important spiritual connection for many children, especially boys. If you think about it, it is not surprising that finding the cusp between safety and destruction can be a place of extraordinary spiritual awareness: where the physical can help release the spiritual, emotional and intellectual domains into pathways that perhaps previously they would not have used. For centuries mystics from the East and West have experimented with starvation, flagellation and substance abuse to help themselves get beyond the 'barrier' of the flesh. I am not for a minute advocating that we encourage our children and young people to even contemplate any of these activities, but instead I am interested in the relationship between the physical and the spiritual.

Many of us have experienced the adrenaline 'whoomph' when we have a near miss in the car, or on a bike. Are the subsequent thankful thoughts on being alive, and concerns for those who might miss us, clearer and more meaningful because of the chemical reactions that have preceded them? Certainly scientific evidence suggests that although neurotransmitters do not speed up sensory processing, they do cause memories to be laid down more richly,[4] so in moments of acute fear or excitement we do have a kind of 'suprasensitivity'. The thoughts and feelings that we have just prior to, during, or just after the event have more significance than others. It is almost as if they are painted in our minds in more vibrant colours.

I wonder, therefore, if this is why boys play 'chicken' across busy roads, or why teenage lads bunny-hop the queue of traffic following a caravan along a single-carriageway road. Are they nipping out, swerving in, narrowly missing the oncoming traffic because the adrenaline buzz helps them to feel truly alive and access those feelings of awe and wonder at a world that could wipe them out in an instant? Perhaps they are also (subconsciously?) testing their knowledge of and reaction to the pain of loved ones left behind.

I was intrigued by this question, but unsure how to find out more. I gave the children one specific choice in the wall charts: 'feeling God's presence when I am scared or excited'. Given the examples talked about previously, I was surprised that this choice did not score more highly for the boys (8%), but not surprised that they did rate it higher than the girls, only 6% of whom felt that it was a helpful spiritual connection for them. It could be that the question was not framed in a way that expresses the 'thrill' of risk; or it could be that some of the children did not register it as a spiritual connection. In the children's church discussions, the children did, however, give a number of examples where doing something risky had helped them to feel God's presence.

Further investigation would need to be undertaken to discover whether the low response from the wall charts was simply because the language used was too religious and did not explain the breadth of experiences in this category, or whether our 'risk-averse' culture is in fact dulling this part of human development in our children and therefore they do not see it as a valid spiritual connection.

I wonder if the lack of 'healthy risk' in children's lives could well have an impact on the other spiritual connections, as play and everything else is organized and controlled for them. It has been argued that although active outdoor play does involve some risks, these are outweighed by the health and developmental benefits.[5] Government consultations show that children do want adults to keep them safe,[6] but other surveys, including the *Good Childhood* report,[7] indicate a strong demand for greater freedom and more places to go. Risk-taking in outdoor play is one of the few ways in which boys can exert some power over their lives, where otherwise they often have very little influence.[8]

Does the church not then have a responsibility to provide them with opportunities to exercise this power in a way that does keep them safe? In the words of Keith White, 'To eliminate risk from the lives of children would be to deny them the very contact with the world for which they strive, and are created.'[9]

I believe that if we do not facilitate children's encounters with the 'thrills and spills' of life on earth, they will start to look for them in darker and more dangerous places. If our boys do not encounter risk in a healthy way, then they will start putting themselves more and more at risk with alcohol and substance abuse, promiscuous sexual activity, gang culture and crime.

What about children who live with a permanent element of risk in their lives? Perhaps they live in an area where it really is risky to walk down the street alone at night; perhaps there is a daily risk of hell breaking loose at home. Is risk then a relevant spiritual connection for them? It could be argued that if it is a permanent, wearing feature of their life, then it should be avoided in their 'safe' places. However, by introducing risks that they can conquer and feel in control of, like an obstacle course or doing a reading in church, that sense of achievement (and the ability to have an effect, rather than being affected) will improve and enhance their emotional and spiritual well-being and help them encounter the safety and security of knowing God. Once again, it is all about knowing the children and young people with whom we work: knowing them from the things they say, from the things we learn about their home life and from the clues they give us non-verbally, but also knowing them through listening to the Holy Spirit as he guides us in discerning the best way to engage with and work with his precious people whom he knows so intimately.

In my discussions with people about this, many have asked, 'So how do we introduce "healthy risk" into the children's lives?' I definitely do not think there is a one-size-fits-all answer. It is about each of us working within, but near the edges of, the policies of our organizations – and taking ourselves to the edges of our own comfort zones as well. In a recent day's teaching on play with my degree students, I introduced some 'free play' activities. At one stage there were two twenty-year-old men chasing each other around the lecture room waving giant pink foam feet at each other. As a short woman, with a degree of responsibility for the room and the other students in it, this was unnerving to say the least! But I had to hold my nerve. They were doing exactly what I had asked them to do, and although the noise and disruption were taking me right to the edge of my comfort zone, it was this noise, disruption, movement and element of risk that made it so exciting and fun for them.

In our risk-averse society, how can we provide children and young people with the opportunity to experience risk and the associated thrill of it, in a way that does not put them or us in unnecessary danger? Many groups and schools are investing in trips to activity centres where the children can take part in supervised rock-climbing or white-water rafting, and these activities do have a part to play. There is nothing to match the grin of someone who, terrified at the bottom, has made it to the top! But for many families and churches, the cost of activities like these is prohibitive.

So how . . . can we introduce activities into our programmes and clubs that give the children the opportunity to explore some 'healthy risk'?

This and this, but not that

Where are the boundaries? Set them out before the game / event starts, and be prepared to enforce them. Boys like to know what's what beforehand. Quite often, as you lay out the boundaries, they will check with what appears to be the precision of a Pharisee exactly what you mean (I guess this is why they not only understand but use the offside rule!). Be prepared to be flexible but firm, and decide where it is appropriate to say 'my game, my rules' or 'your game, your rules'. Once the boys are secure in the boundaries, they will be able

to get the most out of the game and either enjoy it for itself, or interpret the underlying theme you might be getting at.

Vigilance with a blind eye

What you cannot see, you cannot tell them off about! This is not about being negligent or promoting bad behaviour, but rather about giving your boys the freedom that many children no longer get. When I was a child, my brother and I would walk down to the stream a mile or so from our house and spend the day fishing with jam jars. Maybe we were guilty of de-stocking the Sussex waterways, but it was never our intention, and when we climbed over the 'No Entry' signs it was not because we were into sheep-rustling, but because we wanted a private place to have a wee. We had the freedom to make choices and learn from our mistakes, without the 'don't do that' police on our backs.

While the children are in our care, we do need to look after them, but we need to keep asking ourselves the question, 'Am I about to stop them from doing that because it is important, or because what they are doing is making me feel uncomfortable?' I cannot say I am at all enamoured with the idea of rolling in a pile with a group of thirteen-year-old boys (a fact that comes as a mighty relief to them!), but they are, and it is very rarely that the one at the bottom comes out more than slightly ruffled, let alone damaged.

The need for speed

In the same way that disordered eating is not always about food, I do not think that joy-riding is always about cars. If speed was not such an exhilarating sensation, then Formula One and theme parks would not be the multi-million-pound industries they are. Many local councils are investing in skate parks and such like, which are great places for our children and young people to experiment with risk. If these kinds of facilities are not available locally, or your boys are not into it, what about giving them the opportunity to build and race go-karts? Not only are we giving them the opportunity to have control over something and perhaps work as part of a team, but they will also get to experience the thrill of haring down a hill with nothing to brake with apart from the soles of their trainers.

Do it in the dark

By far the most asked-for game with our eight- to eleven-year-olds on a Friday night is 'hide and seek in the dark' in the church. Taking away the ability to see easily is a great way of introducing risk into an activity. How about taking your boys out for a walk in the dark? It is a fantastic opportunity to introduce some 'awe and wonder' as you look at the night sky, or try to spot nocturnal animals. And, if you are town- or city-based, familiar places can still look different and take on a whole new ambience when it is dark. The parks might be locked, but can you get permission to use the local school playground for the evening? Or is there a garden or flat roof that you could use where you could simply lie down on your backs and look at the stars? And if you cannot turn the lights out, what about getting them to do the activity three-legged or blindfolded?

Fire, fire!

This weekend, my son and I built a bonfire. Well, more correctly, he built the bonfire and I helped him to light it. It was the best fun I have had in a long time, and he seemed to enjoy it too. As we sat toasting the bottoms of our wellies near the flames, faces glowing, dipping in and out of nonsense rhymes and songs, I realized what a truly spiritual experience it was. We stared in awe and wonder at the flames as they danced and disappeared into the night sky. We were amazed at the sparks as they exploded and then disappeared as quickly as they came. We thrilled at the possibility that they might get high enough to singe the leaves of the tree above. We congratulated ourselves on our achievement, as this bunch of wood that would not light at first was finally, after several aborted attempts, roaring and crackling. We revelled in the camaraderie of sitting in this circle of light, with our backs to the darkness, safe and warm. And finally we could not resist having another poke with the poking stick, or throwing another twig into the inferno – dangerous, but so much fun!

Side by side

For some boys, one of the greatest risks they will take is to trust someone else with their thoughts and feelings. The great thing about the dark is the anonymity it brings. You may have observed how women and girls often talk face to face, needing the reinforcement of non-verbal communication. There is, however, a tendency for boys and men to converse better when side by side. Any parent of teenagers will tell you that their offspring often divulge the most when sitting in the passenger seat of their car, as if the absence of eyeballs frees them to share whatever it is that is burdening them. Walks in the dark, lying side by side staring at the stars, or sitting next to each other looking into a fire (or watching a match) are all ideal places for boys to have the kinds of conversations that perhaps mean the most to them. These are safe places where they can explore their feelings (perhaps about the risks they have just taken) and their identity formation without having to worry about trying to interpret the non-verbal communication from the person next to them. Be prepared to wait, and do not feel that you have to fill the silences – they are just as important as the words.

Things to think about

- What are you already doing that you could make more 'risky'?
- In what ways can you introduce 'healthy risk' to your programmes and activities?
- How can you help your boys to use risk as a way of engaging with and expressing their spirituality?
- How can we as parents, or those who work with parents, overcome the 'unhealthy fear' that prevents us from allowing our children the freedom we enjoyed when we were their age?

10. I GAME, THEREFORE I AM TECHNOLOGY

"What happened in school today?
Read my blog."[1]

I still get excited when I get a new mobile phone and gaze in wonder at all the things it can do: my children are not nearly so impressed! Boys are surrounded by technology and have been since before they were born. My computer lessons consisted of learning how to write enough 'BASIC' to get a Christmas tree shape to ascend slowly to the top of the screen. Now the infant school down the road has an ICT suite, and children are not taught 'computing', it is an integrated part of the curriculum.

Children in most of the Western world live in a 'multimedia' culture to the extent that those between the ages of eight and eighteen have been called by some 'Generation M' or 'the Media Generation'. I wonder, though, what they are going to call those under eight! Statistics suggest that children are spending on average over forty hours a week engaged with multimedia technology.[2] What we are able to do with a touch of our forefinger would blow the minds of our great-grandparents (if it has not already blown ours); communication is faster, more efficient and more global; images are clearer, more vibrant and more accessible; and if you have not seen or heard it this time round, you can watch it on iPlayer or YouTube. Perhaps the 'World Wide Web' is too limited a phrase to describe something that connects and pulses and reconnects, like synapses in the brain. How exciting, and what endless opportunities! But equally, how do we tread that very thin line between the wonder and potential, the convenience and speed of modern technology, and the dangers that also lie – as with all things human – hidden in the good and the right?

Jesus contextualized his good news with parables about the current culture, and Paul articulated the general principle that ministry is culturally conditioned. While I would not perhaps use the phrase 'multimedia', I do agree that God reveals himself in 'multisensory' ways – through the written and spoken word, through signs and wonders, touch, movement and even tastes and smells. There is no reason to believe, then, that he cannot and does not reveal himself through modern media technology. In fact, there is a lot to be said for using effective communication tools, like multimedia technology, to communicate with children. I am concerned, however, when the technology appears to become the major driver. In 1 Corinthians 9:19–23, Paul does indeed suggest that we should, in one sense, become all things to all people, in order that our differences do not get in the way of the message of the gospel. He does, however, in Romans 12:2, remind us that we are called not to conform to the world, but rather to be transformed by the renewing of our minds by God's Spirit. Jesus himself calls us to be countercultural.[3]

Some writers argue that the proliferation of multimedia in children's lives is actually heralding the end of childhood,[4] believing that 'the diet of violence, sexuality, exploitation and a persistent invitation to consume cannot sustain an autonomous realm of being',[5] and that the boundaries and differences between what is known in childhood and what is known in adulthood are blurring to the point of non-existence. One boy in one of the RE lessons wanted me to read one of his stories before the lesson started. It was very long but extremely well written. What was challenging, though, was that it was all about 'horror cows' who were intent on maiming and killing everything in their path, as the flesh fell from their skeletal forms. The drawing on the front of his 'book' reflected the written imagery. The lesson started, so I did not get a chance to talk to him about what had influenced his subject matter, but I do not think it was just his imagination.

Children are often proficient in the use of technology. I have sometimes returned to my computer at home to find a fully animated PowerPoint display, created by my children, asking 'What's for tea?' I am not convinced, however, that children are always impressed with our attempts to use multimedia in the work that we do! Tim Gill thinks that their proficiency comes from the shrinking freedom for children.[6] In 1971, eight out of ten children aged seven or eight years went to school on their own, and the average seven-year-old was visiting friends or the shops on their own. By 1990, this figure had dropped to less than one in ten, most children not being allowed out on their own until they were ten.[7] Gill argues that growing adult supervision has not quelled the children's appetite for adventure, but has caused them to find it elsewhere, through multimedia activity, and suggests that their 'media-rich bedrooms' have become springboards for exploration and risk-taking and have replaced the dens loved by previous generations. In addition, the statistics for online social networking amongst children show a need for relationship in whatever format it can be had.

The trouble is that, as we face this enormous task of discernment, we are living in a world where so much of what we do is affected by technology, much of which we take for granted. Digital technology allows us to take pictures without film and to listen to radio without hissing. Nanotechnology has a far-reaching influence: for instance, it enables our clothes to feel more comfortable, as well as our phones to be lighter and smaller. In order to prevent this chapter becoming a *'Tomorrow's World* meets *The Gadget Show'*, I will just be concentrating on audio-visual technology and all that this entails, including mobile phones, electronic games, TV and social networking.

Film and TV media

Many researchers and writers have expressed concern at the damage that TV is doing to children's lives, particularly since the amount of time children are spending in front of a TV screen still seems to be increasing (from 2.4 hours a day in 2006, to 2.8 hours a day in 2010). Interestingly, access to multi-channel TV seems to have plateaued and the number of children with their own TV continues to decline gradually: 7 in 10 five- to sixteen-year-olds now have their own TV, down from a high of more than 8 in 10 in 2005. Watching via other platforms does, however, continue to grow. One study has linked TV viewing to obesity and another to aggressiveness, others have related pre-school viewing to hyperactivity

disorders.[8] While there is still debate about the robustness of
these findings, there is a general agreement that it is *excessive*
TV that is the problem. I am not convinced that if children
are spending a high proportion of their 'out of school' hours
watching TV, or audio-visual content via the Internet, as the
statistics suggest, it is therefore always right for them to sit in
front of more multimedia at a Christian club or Sunday school.

Rosemary Duff, the research director of the company
ChildWise responsible for the statistics I am quoting, says that
it is the quality of viewing that has changed. Having lost the
'pay it attention' feel it used to have, where children and indeed
whole families specifically sat down to watch a chosen
programme, audio-visual technology is now so widespread
that it has become part of the background, wherever children
go.[9] In addition, other researchers into the field suggest that
the nature of televisual viewing, which requires the brain
continuously to recognize shapes and patterns to make sense
of the image and therefore leaves little time for analysis, means
that the communication in which the children are engaged
remains shallow and temporary.[10] The combination of both
these factors therefore leads me to have reservations about
whether boys will really engage with Bible stories that are *only*
communicated through this kind of media and whether such
an approach will have a lasting impact on their spirituality.

As far as the children who attended the X:site events were
concerned, watching the re-enactment of Bible stories or
seeing them on screen was not a significant way for them to
hear from God. There also seemed to be no discernible gender
bias in this. Given that children do seem to spend a great deal
of their time watching TV, these results were quite surprising.
There are, perhaps, two particular reasons why. First, there is
still a limited resource base of quality visual biblical materials
available, and so most children will be unable to identify it as

helpful. Second, I think that in their media-rich world, many children actually crave true human interaction and love the rapport created by live storytelling and small-group work.

The writers of *Young Masculinities* reported that the boys they spoke to appeared only to be interested in media representations which were identifiably masculine. Without wishing to criticize specific audio-visual producers, I wonder if there has, up until recently, been a dearth of Bible story videos that could be interpreted by boys as masculine enough to be of interest. The BBC production of *The Passion* portrayed Jesus and his friends as credibly masculine, and an excerpt from this was used at X:site 1 to great effect (although it was difficult to tell whether the boys were more engaged during this than during the retelling of the story which happened later in the programme).

Narrative is incredibly important to all of us, including children. If it was not, then Disney would not be a multi-million-pound operation (although you could argue that it is the marketing of merchandize which has had the greater impact). Children are watching programmes like soaps because they are narratives and display the ups and downs of life in a rich and compellingly exaggerated way. The downside of soaps and programmes like them is that while the children are absorbed in the drama of the story, they are also absorbing some values and attitudes that are not what we would want for them.

Gaming

There is a continuing debate about the dangers of gaming. Some argue that incidents like the killing of Jamie Bulger are solely due to the 'evil' influence of visual media. Others believe that for many children, and boys in particular, new technology has given them unprecedented and myriad ways to express themselves and communicate with others. So how do we discern what is positive and what is harmful, what can open new opportunities for our boys and what can shut down their potential? Unfortunately, there is no catch-all formula, a set of rules that will work indiscriminately across the board. Once again the secret is to know the boys with whom you work – to know what makes them tick, what gets them excited and where their limitations are. It is also important to have an open mind and be prepared not to dismiss or encourage something without having really assessed its potential, whether that is good or bad.

The term 'gaming' can cover a wide spectrum of activities from adrenaline-fuelled cyber-racing against mates to solitary brain exercises. A couple of the boys from the church group did put 'playing on my DS' as a way in which they would like to worship God. At X:site 6, one boy put 'when I play on my DS' as his response to the 'I feel closest to God when . . . ' and 'I feel I belong when . . . ' posters. This initiated an interesting discussion, when a girl who had noticed this told me what he had put and asked me to affirm her belief that this was wrong. I asked why she felt that it was wrong, and she could not answer. We then talked about the sensation of playing on a DS or a Wii, and how this might make you feel close to God.

Some would argue, based on various studies,[11] that because the two hemispheres of a male brain are not as connected as those of a female brain, boys actually need more time to move from one activity to another. But when it comes to gaming, they seem to be able to process numerous stimuli simultaneously. I am sure that many of you have been in the situation where you have been playing some kind of electronic game, and your seven-year-old playmate seamlessly copes with the various obstacles that are thrown across the track, when you did not see them coming at all! And oh, their joy when they beat you! One of the other key themes of gaming is the competition. 'High score' boards can hold a lot of pleasure for some boys and indeed a lot of pain for others.

Competition and rewards

Some models of children's ministry use structure and graduated award systems as frameworks for scripture memorization and biblical instruction, using a principle based on Romans 8:29a which argues that memorizing Bible verses puts them within the life of a child in such a way that the Holy Spirit can use these verses for transformation. But only 6% of the girls and 6% of the boys who attended the X:site events chose 'learning Bible verses and thinking about them later' as a way in which they felt they heard from God. What is interesting is the variation of responses from the different events around the country, indicating, perhaps, that it is the way in which the Bible verses are taught that has an impact on whether the children believe it affects their spirituality.

Some writers are critical of the use of competition and reward,[12] believing that children are vulnerable, to their very core, to the expectations and messages of love and approval that come from those on whom the children depend. 'Affective messages of approval and disapproval can register powerfully on the very finely calibrated scale of self-worth taking form in the child's inmost heart.'[13]

I wonder, then, if for some boys the need to get the verse right, to win the approval of the group leaders, and the fear of disapproval for not being able to memorize the scripture, actually can become a hurdle to the memorization and/or the scripture having an impact on their thoughts and feelings about its content. My concern is that, if the learning is only 'cognitive' and not 'affective', learned and not understood, what happens when reality is not logical or straightforward and when 'bad things happen to good people'? I am not convinced that for all children, particularly those who might trail behind in standardized cognitive development like some boys, or who have had negative experiences in the classroom, this methodology is going to have a hugely positive impact on their spirituality.

I do, however, believe that a sense of achievement and the satisfaction gained from having got something 'right' is significant in the spiritual formation of many children, particularly boys. It is clear from the 'I feel . . .' posters that the boys get some of their spiritual connection from a sense of achievement and success. Without further investigation it is impossible to tell whether this is coming from their own sense of worth, or from their parents, or how much it is influenced by the teaching they have received at school or at Christian events like Sunday school and X:site, but I am concerned that so much of it does appear to be conditional.

In one of the RE lessons, I did a simple activity called 'Bible Treasure Trove' where the children were given several Bible verses and had to decide which ones might help a Christian to make a decision, in the dilemmas that I then read out. Those who were able to give me an answer first, or persuade me it was the best and why, were then given a chocolate coin to lay on top of that verse. I had chosen this kind of activity because it was the last day of term before the Easter holidays, and I wanted to do something light and fun as well as instructional. I was amazed at how both classes, and especially the boys, completely engaged with this activity, but I am ambivalent about whether this had an impact on their spirituality. What intrigues me is the question of how much they were motivated by the chocolate and how much they were motivated by persuading me they were right and getting public approbation.

Emailing and social networking

For a few years I have been involved with a transition programme for Year 6 youngsters, 'It's Your Move', where we spend about an hour with them using the story of Joseph or David to think through the issues of moving up to secondary school. I have been struck over the years by how the things that the children are concerned about have not changed, but the means of doing them have. In our discussions on communication, letters and postcards have been replaced by emails, and calling round for your mate has been usurped by calling your mate on a mobile.

It was also interesting how, this year in particular, what the children were telling us bore out the national statistics that suggest that social networking is the main online activity for five- to sixteen-year-olds, with Facebook and YouTube being the favourite websites across boys and girls, younger and older children. This is possible partly because the number of five- to sixteen-year-olds owning their own PC or laptop is now 6 in 10, and half of all seven- to sixteen-year-olds can access the Internet in their own room. These are national statistics, so there are going to be areas around the country where this is not a true reflection of what is going on in many homes, but the reality is that, particularly with the advent of Smartphones, more and more boys will have access to this kind of technology.

Whether we lobby Facebook to put more stringent age tests on profile applicants, or parents to be stricter, or whatever, the fact of the matter is that the children we are working with are using these sites in their millions – and it is not all bad; in fact for some boys it might be all good. Boys do like to talk, but sometimes when faced with a more threatening situation, like a group of girls, they can clam up for fear of not being as articulate or forthright as the rest of the group, or simply not wanting to share the stuff that makes them feel vulnerable. Online chatting, or texting, gives them an opportunity to have a conversation about some really deep stuff, without the embarrassment of anyone seeing their stutters or blushes, and through a medium that allows them to phrase what they are saying carefully, and even delete a sentence if they are not ready to share it yet. The question, of course, is how we keep these tools good and safe, and do not allow them to become the only method of communication that our boys can use!

 So how . . . do we help boys to engage with and express their spirituality through multimedia technology?

Message me

For many boys, an opportunity to 'chew the cud' online or via text about things that matter to them may be a real boost to their ability to make meaning, and your availability, albeit cyber, may be a lifeline to their sense of belonging. It is important to think very carefully about how you are going to engage with the children and young people over the Internet, and to agree a policy and an accountability structure with all your leaders. Many children's and youth workers have two profiles or phones, one for work and one for private use. Try to keep your communication in the public domain (e.g. on Facebook communicate via walls rather than messages), but if that is not possible, cut and paste information into Word documents and keep records of exchanges. Perhaps you could start a chat room which the children know will be open at particular times on particular days and in which they can share not just with you but also with their other friends. In this way they can exercise their 'Internet wings' safely and give you further opportunities to come alongside them on their discipleship journey.

For the 'It's Your Move' transition programme, we set up a website where the children could send in messages to their classmates and post questions to an agony aunt that they did not want to ask in front of their class. The system meant that it was completely anonymous, unless they said otherwise, and provided an excellent vehicle for discussing some of their fears about friends and members of the opposite sex.

Watch it!

The implications of research into neural activity is that as the speed of children's thinking increases, so their emotional intelligence will suffer. If spirituality is about belonging and making sense of the world, then perhaps we should be encouraging children to reflect more deeply on the films and TV programmes that they are watching and the feelings they evoke. Why does *Tracy Beaker*[14] make them feel sad? Why do the lion, giraffe, zebra and hippo stick together in *Madagascar*?[15] What do they understand about their family and their place in it from watching *The Simpsons*?

Try to watch some of the programmes the children are watching on a regular basis. Not only does this mean that you will understand what they are talking about, but it also gives you the material to ask the right kind of questions that will help deepen their thoughts about what they have been watching. Remember that they are not just watching children's programmes, so make sure you cover a reasonably broad spectrum and consider the values that they are picking up from what they watch.

I did it!

Think about how you can provide the boys with the opportunity to have a sense of achievement. It may require some complex planning, or it may be something very simple. In January we revamped our attendance prizes into 'sticker passports' for our children's church. The idea was that every time they attended they got a sticker, and when they had ten stickers they got to choose a sweet or gift from the box. Thirty stickers, and they got a more valuable gift presented to them in church. This is not a new concept, but it is much loved! I am amazed at how many boys will follow me around with a smile and a completed row, perhaps a minor achievement – coming along with your parents – but an achievement nevertheless.

Game on!

Your boys are already gaming: so game with them! First, to find out what it is they are enjoying about this activity – is it adrenaline, is it achievement, is it connectivity, is it the visual image? Second, to help you identify where the spiritual connection can be enhanced. And third, to identify what you can do about it. Can you enhance a sense of belonging by linking gamers online or creating 'gaming' events? One local youth work agency has recently spent thousands of pounds equipping half a dozen youth cafés with Wii games, hoping to attract young men to their activities. In one sense it does work – normally someone (and it is not always a boy) is standing in front of the large screen engaging with the images on it.

As we have already seen, achievement is important for children and young people, whether it be sporting, academic, behavioural or on a virtual race track. If, however, so much gaming is done on an individual basis, how can we break down the barriers of isolation that this creates? One possibility is to make the game more performance- or team-orientated. At a recent youth event, a 'Guitar Hero' Wii game competition was held where several heats offered two contestants the chance to battle it out. The semi-finals and final were held on the stage and watched by everyone else, busy cheering on their friends and swapping their own scores and techniques.

Things to think about

- What technology do your boys have access to?
- What technology should you be introducing to your club / group / activities?
- What policies do you need to create and communicate to keep the children and team safe online?
- How can you help the boys use the technology they are engaging with to explore their sense of belonging and meaning-making?

PART THREE
GO AND DO LIKEWISE

GO AND DO LIKEWISE

Many boys and young men are conscious of the perception that they are a 'problem' for society, but despite this show a willingness to engage in the struggle to make themselves heard and seen as they are: full of fun, energy, feeling and spirituality. Remember, there are many ways of 'doing boy'. Listen to and watch your boys to find out what they are into, and how best you can use their energy and passion to help them connect with God in new and exciting ways. Do not be frightened of getting out of the box, but instead be prepared to put in place activities and events that give boys the opportunity to engage with their spirituality and faith, through thinking, feeling, seeing and doing.

Play, play and play

In my original list of spiritual connections I had 'play' as a single connection, but over time I have come to realize that actually it has an impact on many of the other ways in which children connect with God and therefore should feature in all aspects of what we offer to boys. Play not only enables the acquisition of information, it also encourages flexibility and may even help the brain to retain plasticity, that is, its ability to change and grow in response to outside stimuli.[1] In the chapter entitled 'Our Father' we thought about the importance in boys' lives of adults who are prepared to play. In 'Muscles and mayhem' we looked at the importance of rough-and-tumble play. 'Make it go away' points out how play can be an antidote to pain, while 'Thrills and spills' encourages us to take risks in our play with boys. It would appear, then, that 'play' is not necessarily a spiritual connection in its own right, but something that should be a fundamental part of all the connections.

So learn from your boys the importance of play and encourage them in their play, whether that be imaginative play, word play, free play, silent play, group play, structured play, play in solitude, creative play or rough-and-tumble play. Be creative in the ways you can support them and allow them to take risks that will stretch their understanding of this world and their God, who took the ultimate risk of giving them free will so that they can choose to connect with him. Get them involved in the life of your church, school or group, giving them responsibilities that help them to grow in their connection with the people around them and offer them a sense of purpose and meaning through value.

Tell them stories using a variety of techniques, including active dramatization and introspective Godly Play style stories. Include periods of time for space and reflection. Utilize the stories that make up their lives and who they are, helping them to see the patterns and rituals that provide them with opportunities to connect with God in silence and in words. Fill their world with colour, beauty and vibrant visual imagery that enables communication on a number of levels and not just through words.

Do not limit your boys to noise and activity, but offer them opportunities for silence and space, and work on ideas that equip them to pray quietly on their own. They might not always verbalize their prayers, so in group settings create rituals that allow them to pray without speaking. Remember, some boys might not want to talk about their spiritual life with others, but this does not mean that they do not have one! Our job is to provide genuine relationships that pay attention to their verbal and non-verbal communication and are intent on journeying alongside our boys. We need to be willing to take some risks too and allow those dragonflies to soar over the water, even if it looks a little scary to us.

It is a huge privilege to play a small part in the spiritual and faith development of a boy as he grows into manhood. We cannot do this in isolation, but as part of a team of parents and family, teachers, friends and peers. Sometimes that might require us to rattle a few cages as we try to open the eyes of those around us, including the church, to the possibilities as well as the responsibilities. And so, as it is our duty and joy at all times and in all places to worship the triune God who longs for our connection with him, it is also our duty and joy at all times and in all places to point our boys in the direction of that God, and to give them opportunities to make connections that are healing, restoring, challenging and ascendant: to find, clean, repair and celebrate their 'God goggles'.

Every boy I met during my period of study, and continue to meet in my work, has a different set of spiritual connections. Some hold a wide range of connections lightly, others use a couple deeply and religiously. The key to helping our boys to engage with and express their spirituality is to listen to them and to journey with them. That way, sometimes when we least expect it, we will see that glorious dragonfly flit into our view and hover over the water, and something will change in us as we watch it soar and dart and reflect the sunlight.

APPENDIX 1: STATISTICS ON BOYS' CHILDHOOD EXPERIENCES

	Age	Ratio or percentage	
		Boys	**Girls**
About 1 in 10 British children were identified as having a mental disorder[1]	5–10	5	3
	11–15	13	10
Permanent exclusions from school[2]		5	1
Placement in special school[3]		2	1
Diagnosed with autism[4]		4	1
Diagnosed with Asperger's syndrome[5]		9	1
Found guilty of, or cautioned for, an indictable offence[6]	10–17	4	1
Key Stage 2 SATS, 11-year-olds achieving Level 4 and above	English	70%	80%
	Mathematics	71%	70%
	Science	87%	88%

APPENDIX 2: THE CREATION OF THE SPIRITUAL CONNECTIONS LIST

First I compared the 'Tellegen scale'[1] to Hay's and Nye's definitions of 'spiritual sensitivities'. Although the Tellegen scale was originally devised in 1974 (and revised in 1981) to measure a person's susceptibility to hypnosis, it has been identified as an effective investigative tool for people who have had unusual, intense spiritual experiences, because it measures things like 'a heightened sense of reality' and 'an empathically altered sense of self'. While the writers themselves may not completely agree with my interpretation of their terminology, I think that there is sufficient overlap to show the importance of the use of *imagination, external stimulation* and *thinking* in spiritual engagement.

In their book *The Shaping of Things to Come*, Frost and Hirsch talk about the appeal of the Burning Man festival in the Nevada desert.[2] They identify six key elements that they believe make the experience so attractive to the thousands of people who attend, and I thought it would be interesting to see how these relate to the other models. Once again relationship is important, with *belonging* being the first element, but there is also a focus on the stimulation of the senses through *sensuality*, *celebration* and *survival*. *Empowerment*, where no-one is deemed to be without a talent, is also considered important. What is intriguing is the inclusion of *liminality*. The word 'liminal' stems from the Latin word for 'threshold' and signifies transition, implying change and *rites of passage*.

Another useful model was that written by Geraint Davies which describes the different qualities a school should be expecting to develop in children when referring to their spiritual understanding.[3] These are very outcome-based, but do show the importance of the *relational* aspect of spirituality as well as the *internal 'thinking' processes* required to develop these.

Gary Thomas based his ideas on an understanding of the Myers Briggs personality types, and devised a number of 'spiritual temperaments' as a way to explain, he says, how we each love God differently.[4] However, he does make the distinction between personality temperament and spiritual temperament, and in some informal research amongst my students it was interesting to discover that many of them preferred a spiritual connection and/or a style of worship seemingly at odds with their Myers-Briggs personality type.

With these models in mind, and my concern that there was something missing for those who are more physical in their spirituality, I created a list of ways in which I believe children engage with and express their spirituality. Initially I considered calling them 'encounters', but felt that this implied something more concrete than some of the abstract concepts that spirituality covers. The term 'approaches' was also considered, but again this implies a definite action and motive from the individual having the spiritual experience, which is not always the case. I therefore settled for the term 'connections', as this implies a two-way process with no set initiator, and allows for the fact that the strength of that process can vary, perhaps being as slender as a spider's web attached to a washing line, or as strong as an anchor sunk into the seabed.

Relational	Aesthetic	Intrapersonal	Active	Ritualistic
Relationship	The arts (creativity)	Thinking and philosophizing	'Good works' or service	Silence
Pain and loss	Senses	Mystery and wonder	Risk-taking	Prayer
Story or narrative	Nature		Play	Ritual
Conversation	Music			
Touch				
Humour				

For the purposes of this book, these various spiritual connections have been grouped under ten headings, as explored in part 2.

APPENDIX 3: THE RESEARCH PROJECT

Scripture Union X:site events

Research was carried out at six X:site events around England.[1] As these events welcome a large number of children for a relatively short space of time, I was keen to find a methodology that created similar information to that of a questionnaire but also:

- was appealing to the children (and therefore encouraged their participation);
- took as little time as possible and could easily be fitted into a busy programme;
- incorporated a method of translatable data collection.

Each chosen event was therefore sent a 'research pack' with all the resources to elicit the children's responses through the two 'wall charts' and three 'I feel . . .' posters described in the 'Ways of listening' chapter. Information was gathered from 150 girls and 140 boys between the ages of seven and eleven. It was not appropriate to find out how many of the children were churched or unchurched, but my perception of the results is that the children were predominantly churched, or at least had a very good understanding of religious language.

Wall charts

Each wall chart consisted of twelve A3 sheets of brightly coloured card, printed with a possible answer and a picture representing it. These were strung on a ribbon along a wall so that the children could quickly annotate the chart in between other activities in the programme.

The most popular way to hear from God, with about a third of both the girls and boys expressing a preference, was through 'singing and music'. For some this is maybe through their own musical activity, but for many it is probably an expression of the connection with God they experience when joining in singing at church and at events like X:site.

'Doing something that represents my prayers' was the least popular choice for both girls and boys. This could be because the card was bright pink and therefore unattractive to boys who have been taught to gender-stereotype colours, but if that is the case, why was the reverse not true for the girls? Given some of the other results, I do have reservations about how much the children understood of what this statement actually meant. Perhaps it would be more helpful to bear in the mind the responses for 'praying in a small group' and 'praying on my own' as well.

A fifth of the boys felt that 'looking at pictures or at God's creation' and 'acting out Bible stories' were helpful, which shows the importance of a visual and narrative connection, although 'watching Bible stories' was less favoured. Maybe there is limited experience of quality visual biblical materials available, hence most were unable to identify it as helpful.

I was surprised that 'feeling God's presence when I am scared or excited' did not score more highly for the boys. It could be that the question was not framed in a way that expresses the 'thrill' of risk, or it could be that some of the children did not register it as a spiritual connection because it is the perceived *absence* of God that makes them scared.

For nearly a third of the boys, 'praying on my own' was their favourite way to respond to God. 'Making things and being creative' was also popular across the board, with the boys ranking it alongside 'looking after God's creation'. Again this shows the variety of responses from the boys, and perhaps dispels the myth that 'boys don't like crafts'. 'Thinking and making plans' was the girls' least favourite way to respond to God, but 10% of the boys did choose this as an option. Their least favourite response was, perhaps not surprisingly, 'writing something'.

When the results were analysed by categorizing the responses according to the spiritual connections, there was very little difference between those for the boys and those for the girls, with both genders showing a preference for the active and aesthetic connections, closely followed by the relational. However, 14% of the boys' (as opposed to 11% of the girls') responses showed the ritualistic connections to be important, reflecting the strength of the emphasis on praying alone, described above.

'I feel . . . ' posters

The 'I feel . . . ' posters described in the 'Ways of listening' chapter were designed to encourage the children to think about more general spiritual experiences. This produced some very interesting results. Although the anonymity probably produced better responses, it is a shame that the responses were not labelled, as it would have been fascinating to talk further with the children about why they had responded in the way they did. As I recorded the children's completion of the 'I feel . . . ' statements, I noticed several themes emerging. These were used to categorize responses for ease of analysis.

'I feel closest to God when . . . '

Perhaps not surprisingly, a third of the children mentioned prayer as a means of feeling closest to God. What is interesting is that, although more of the girls mentioned places, and predominantly church, as being a factor, nearly half of the boys focused on prayer, silence or being on their own. It is also significant that achievement either academically or through sport was also seen as a means of feeling close to God by more boys than girls. Although some of the girls mentioned it, none of the boys suggested that family were key in helping them in this area, indicating again that perhaps their spirituality is deeply held but not lightly shared. The girls were much more able to use other means like music, art and reading the Bible to feel closer to God and express this.

The large number of statements relating to prayer and attendance at church mean that the 'ritualistic' spiritual connections are rather heavily represented. But even if we took out church attendance and put it with relationship and belonging (which other analysis has shown is probably more the case), we still see silence (or being on my own / alone) and prayer as key, particularly for the boys. The relational spiritual connections account for well over a third of the total responses, but are more significant for the girls than for the boys.

'I feel I matter when . . . '

The relational spiritual connections account for nearly half of the responses when it comes to 'mattering', with not just relationship and belonging being important, but also conversation and story – although once again it is the girls who express this more than the boys. For the boys, 17% of the statements show the importance of achievement and 12% the importance of feelings in helping them to work through this existential issue. The active connections were also important, particularly in terms of acts of service and play.

'I feel I belong when . . . '

Not surprisingly, people were once again a major feature of the statements the children made about belonging, with the relational spiritual connections accounting for nearly 60% of the responses. Eight of the children specifically talked about their relationship with God (aside from generally talking about prayer), and although specifically under 'place', I think that the 38 responses which talked about belonging at church, school and at home are actually reflecting the relationships rather than the buildings. What was also significant for the boys was the opportunity and experience of participating, whether that was simply being allowed to join in, or was more specifically to do with being part of a particular team or sport. They also expressed the importance of feelings and prayer again.

Research in an Anglican children's church

Due to various factors, the children's church needed to make some changes. The research project, therefore, sought not only to discover insights about my hypothesis, but also to improve our practice. I designed a pictorial questionnaire which asked the children to show their preferences for activities under four main headings and to complete some 'I feel . . .' phrases. A 'new and improved' version of the children's church was launched in January 2009. After a few weeks, a meeting was held to discuss the outcomes of the changes. It was generally agreed that the new format was working well.

In March 2009 I held small, videoed focus groups with the children, as part of our Sunday morning activities. I used an A4 version of the 'Ways I like to respond to God' wall charts as the starting point of our discussion, with the intention of seeing whether their responses were different from those given on the questionnaires. In general the focus groups worked well, with the children freely expressing their opinions about what they felt were helpful ways for them to respond to God.

The groups were then asked to put the sheets in order of importance. The range of responses to this request was really interesting. Some groups interpreted this as importance to themselves personally, and certain individuals were unwilling to compromise; other groups worked together to compile a consensual list; yet others interpreted the question to mean what might be important in general (i.e. in the eyes of adults and church leaders) rather than their own preferences.

Unfortunately, due to the nature of children's church attendance, very few of the children who attended on this day were the same as those children who had completed the questionnaires. This meant that comparison of the two was sketchy. It was, however, interesting to see that in discussion many of the children expressed different opinions from those written on the questionnaires, and were much more keen to form a consensus in the group than to be adamant about their own preferences. Perhaps this suggests that if they are having fun and are engaged in activity with their friends, children are happy to go along with and get something out of activities that might not be their first preference.

Research during RE lessons

I undertook a term of RE lessons with two Year 6 classes of mixed gender, mixed ability and mixed faith in a local junior school. They were two lively classes, which is only to be expected at this point in their school career, on a Friday afternoon! As the research was not conducted alongside the activity, but as part of it, there were various elements that were completely outside my control, but which had a huge impact on the attitude, attention span and feelings of the children in the class. For instance, prior to Lesson Six the children had spent the week doing SATS tests and had hotdogs for lunch as an end-of-exams treat. I do believe, however, that this is a positive factor in the research project, as it means that the findings were made in a 'real' situation and, therefore, could be applied in other less than perfect environments!

Although working with Year 6 classes is often tricky, particularly in Aylesbury where the pressures of the 11-plus exam add a further distortion to the motivation of these children and adolescents, I believe that it was really important to work with this age group. Not only are they great fun as they sway between childhood and teendom, but they are also at the end of the age range that typifies high levels of report of religious and spiritual experiences.[2] Hay believes that this downturn in spiritual expression is mainly the responsibility of induction to the 'sceptical tradition of the Enlightenment' brought about via their scientific education.[3] It is possible that this was the reason why many of the children approached the subjects with caution, looking for a right or wrong answer. However, this caution could, as easily, have been caused by the classroom environment, where teachers are looking for answers that reflect the transfer of information.

While 'spiritual development' is something that is supposed to be assessed across the curriculum by Ofsted,[4] for many schools RE lessons are the focus of opportunities for the children to reflect on their own beliefs and practices and on those of others. Lessons, by their very nature, are still heavily biased towards a transfer of facts and propositional and technical knowledge, and the main purpose of the lessons I took was to inform the children of the basic tenets of the Christian faith. It was therefore very difficult to assess how much, if any, spiritual development occurred as part of these lessons. I was, however, able to see tentative examples of children expressing values, insights and engagements that indicated some level of spirituality.

The intention was to fulfil the requirements of the curriculum, using as many different techniques as possible, to see which ones the children responded to best. This included using fine art pictures,[5] storytelling, Godly Play techniques, question-and-answer sessions, percussion and competition. Each technique reflected some of the 'spiritual connections' being tested, and was chosen to fit the curriculum material covered for that session. Although the term was loosely planned beforehand, as the children informed me of their preferences with the 'yes/no' cards, so the lessons were geared more and more to their requirements. This meant that the statements made at the end of each session, relating to the techniques and content in that session, did not end up covering the full range that I had hoped. In fulfilling the requirements of action research and improving my practice, I started to diminish the range of information that I could get for the research!

I asked the children to complete an anonymous form to see how much of their responses was affected by membership of

a faith community. What is encouraging about the results is
that the children seemed to feel free to express the reality of
their situation, rather than what they thought they should say.
Many of the children who attend a mosque, church or temple
said that they did not have a faith; and many of the children
who said they had a faith indicated that they do not worship
anywhere. For one or two of the children, this paper caused
a problem. One boy circled everything, and one said, 'My
mum was a Christian except she doesn't believe in God. I kind
of believe in God.' There seemed to be a clear indication that,
despite the fact that many of the children do not see themselves as engaging in 'worship' regularly, if at all, they still
believe in and/or engage with something. There was also an
indication that in the classroom, religion may well be a barrier
to spiritual development. There was certainly evidence that
some children did not engage with the lessons in the same
way as the others because it was about Christianity, while
others were giving 'pat' answers that perhaps belonged to the
doctrine of their faith, rather than coming from their own
experience or understanding.

APPENDIX 4: MICHAEL ANTHONY'S FOUR PERSPECTIVES OF CHILDREN'S MINISTRY

In his book entitled *Perspectives on Children's Spiritual Formation*, Michael Anthony explores how different models of children's ministry can enhance children's spiritual and faith development. He introduces a matrix which gives a continuum between 'doing' and 'watching' on the horizontal axis, and 'feeling' and 'thinking' on the vertical axis, and then suggests four models of children's ministry that typify the type of spiritual engagement in each quadrant, asking experts in these ministries to suggest why they are successful and propose theological, ethical and psychological reasons for their use.

What is perhaps more helpful is that the proponents from each quadrant then critique the others, creating an interesting and thought-provoking dialogue. Unfortunately, as the book is American, all the examples chosen are based in the USA, although some of them are used (in diluted forms) in the UK.

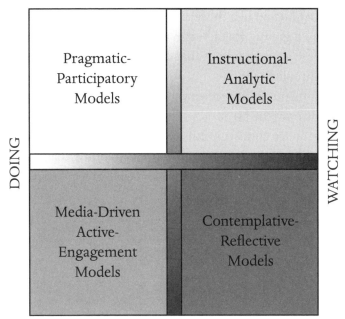

If, as many of the definitions of spirituality suggest, spirituality is about how we think and feel about ourselves, God and others, then a model that examines these two important methods of engagement seems a sensible place to start. As part of the research project, therefore, I compared the data to where it seemed to fit into the four quadrants, with the following results.

Pragmatic-participatory findings (for instance, Scripture Union 'Light' material)

- Elements of this model appear to be popular amongst the children who attended the X:site events.
- The singing and music element, so strong in this model, is slightly more highly favoured by the girls.

- The variety of reactions across the X:sites indicates that other factors like the leaders and peer pressure could have a greater impact than anticipated.
- There is an argument that drama could enhance boys' spirituality.
- Acting out Bible stories was more popular among the girls than the boys.
- There are concerns that a fast-paced programme which emphasizes cognitive understanding does not give the children the space they need to reflect and wonder.

Instructional-analytic findings (for instance, highly structured Bible learning with rewards)

- Cognitive activities do work for some boys, but:
  - they are probably better done in single-sex groups;
  - they should not involve too much reading or writing down.
- Boys do like to talk about things that matter to them.
- Active games are an important part of the lives of many children.
- A sense of achievement is important in helping children make sense of belonging and mattering.

Media-driven active-engagement findings (for instance, Bible teaching delivered by DVD)

- Boys did show a slightly higher preference for visual and multimedia elements. Other statistics show that boys are using multimedia more than girls in general.
- Some boys expressed gaming as a spiritual activity, and this needs further investigation.

- Perhaps children separate their multimedia activities from their spiritual life and work needs to be done on making connections for them.
- Much is written about the harm multimedia can do to children's lives and their development, but the reality is that this is their world. Further work needs to be done on using what is 'good' in what the children watch, and encouraging children and parents to think about other ways of living too.

Contemplative-reflective findings (for instance, Godly Play)

- Evidence suggests that even in a school environment, elements of the contemplative-reflective approach can work.
- Boys expressed preferences for activities that give them time to reflect quietly and pray on their own.
- Story and narrative are important to children and helpful in meaning-making.
- Wondering rather than questioning with the expectation of a right answer may give more children the chance to interact with the subject matter.
- Structure, routine and repetition are helpful to some boys.
- Making things and being creative is a popular spiritual response.
- Children want an opportunity to express their spirituality and/or faith through service to others.

A new model

While Anthony's model was helpful as a framework for reviewing children's spiritual connections, it does not, I feel, cover the full spectrum of experiences and methods of engagement that boys require if they are to maximize their potential to connect with God and relate to those around them. My conclusion from the research evidence, and my experience, is that to concentrate on one model of ministry limits the opportunities for children to engage with and express their spirituality, and therefore could lead to many of our boys not only opting out of church but also not developing fully in their faith and their humanity.

I am therefore proposing a new model which turns Anthony's matrix on its side and makes it a base for a pyramid (see below), to illustrate that the pinnacle of our engagement with children, and our efforts to develop their faith and their spirituality, requires us to use the strengths of all four elements of thinking, feeling, doing and watching. Play becomes, figuratively speaking, a band around the whole pyramid.

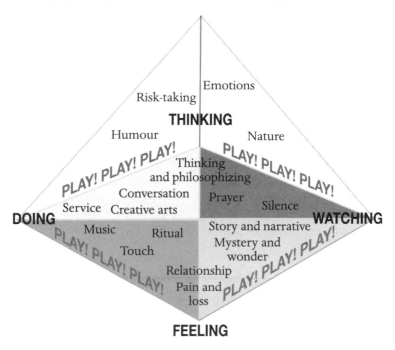

NOTES

A spiritual spectrum?

1. T. Hart, *The Secret Spiritual World of Children* (California: New World Library, 2003).
2. G. Mursell (ed.), *The Story of Christian Spirituality* (Oxford: Lion Publishing, 2001).
3. K. Copsey, *From the Ground Up: Understanding the Spiritual World of the Child* (Oxford: Bible Reading Fellowship, 2005).
4. D. Hay and R. Nye, *Spirit of the Child* (London: HarperCollins, 1998).
5. E. McCreery, 'Talking to Young Children about Things Spiritual', in R. Best (ed.), *Education, Spirituality and the Whole Child* (London: Cassell, 1996).
6. Oxford CYM is one of the regional centres for CYM (Centre for Youth Ministry) which delivers undergraduate and postgraduate qualifications in Children, Family, Youth, Schools and Community Work.
7. G. Gutiérrez, *We Drink from Our Own Wells: The Spiritual Journey of a People*, 20th anniversary ed. (Maryknoll: Orbis, 2003).
8. H. Gardner, *Multiple Intelligences*, 2nd ed. (New York: Basic Books, 2006).
9. A phrase growing in popularity and used most recently by Pridmore in his chapter on salvation in A. Richards and P. Privett (eds.), *Through the Eyes of a Child: New Insights in Theology from a Child's Perspective* (London: Church House Publishing, 2009).
10. See, for instance, Hay and Nye, *Spirit of the Child*.
11. See, for instance, http://www.cofe.anglican.org/info/statistics/2007provisionalattendance; *Baptist Times*, Thursday 27 September 2007, p. 17.
12. See, for instance, D. Nettle, 'Empathizing and Systemizing: What Are They, and What Do They Contribute to Our Understanding of Psychological Sex Differences?', *British Journal of Psychology* 98 (2007), pp. 237–255; Davis et al., 'Meaning, Purpose and Religiosity in At-Risk Youth: The Relationship between Anxiety and Spirituality', *Journal of Psychology and Theology*, 21 (2003).
13. Copsey, *From the Ground Up*.

Ways of listening

1. W. Blake, 'Nurse's Song', *Songs of Innocence and Experience* (1794).
2. Wehr talks about the problems of 'projective identification', where the recipient of the projection (in this case the child) takes it in, identifies with it and acts it out, in D. S. Wehr, 'Spiritual Abuse: When Good People Do Bad Things', in P. Young-Eisendrath and M. E. Miller, *The Psychology of Mature Spirituality: Integrity, Wisdom, Transcendence* (Hove: Routledge, 2000), p. 56.
3. H. Gardner, *Multiple Intelligences*, 2nd ed. (New York: Basic Books, 2006).
4. See, for instance, V. Morrow and M. Richards, 'The Ethics of Social Research with Children: An Overview', *Children and Society* 10 (2) (1996), pp. 90–103.

1. Our Father

1. For discussions on the role of parents in the development of children's deity images, see L. B. Brown, *The Psychology of Religious Belief* (London: Academic Press, 1987); A. Rizzuto, *The Birth of the Living God* (Chicago: University of Chicago Press, 1980).
2. B. Beit-Hallahmi and M. Argyle, 'God as a Father-Projection: The Theory and the Evidence', *British Journal of Medical Psychology* 48 (1975), pp. 71–75.
3. See, for instance, J. W. Fowler, *Stages of Faith: The Psychology of Human Development and the Quest for Meaning* (USA: Harper and Row, 1981); and *Faith Development and Pastoral Care* (Philadelphia: Fortress Press, 1987); J. H. Westerhoff, *Bringing Up Children in the Christian Faith* (Minneapolis: Winston Press, Inc., 1980).
4. See *The Fatherhood Bibliography* compiled by CARE, 2007.
5. S. Frosh, A. Phoenix and R. Pattman, *Young Masculinities: Understanding Boys in Contemporary Society* (Basingstoke: Palgrave Macmillan, 2001).
6. D. Andrews, *Compassionate Community Work: An Introductory Course for Christians* (Carlisle: Piquant Editions, 2006).
7. Research done by Simon Baron-Cohen and his colleagues looked at two quotients: empathizing (the drive to identify another person's emotions and thoughts) and systemizing (the drive to analyse or construct systematic relationships in non-social domains). They discovered that although both sexes showed a variation in both dimensions, on average women were higher than men in empathizing and men had a higher systemizing quotient.

See D. Nettle, 'Empathizing and Systemizing: What Are They, and What Do They Contribute to Our Understanding of Psychological Sex Differences?', *British Journal of Psychology* 98 (2007), pp. 237–255.

8. In epidemiological research, Wing found that among people with high-functioning autism or Asperger's syndrome there were as many as fifteen times as many males as females. On the other hand, when she looked at individuals with learning difficulties as well as autism, the ratio of boys to girls was closer to 2:1. This would suggest that, while females are less likely to develop autism, when they do they are more severely impaired. See L. Wing, 'Sex Ratios in Early Childhood Autism and Related Conditions', *Psychiatry Research* 5 (1981), pp. 129–137. For more information visit www.autism.org.uk.

9. Frosh et al., *Young Masculinities*.

10. See, for instance, M. Buber, *I and Thou* (New York: Scribner, 1970), pp. 78–80; and Sterne (2002), cited in K. Copsey, *From the Ground Up: Understanding the Spiritual World of the Child* (Oxford: Bible Reading Fellowship, 2005), p. 94.

11. G. Thomas, *Sacred Pathways* (Grand Rapids: Zondervan, 2002).

12. See www.family-time.co.uk.

13. See www.scriptureunion.org.uk/Families/Parents/SurvivalSkillsforChristianParents.

2. Muscles and mayhem

1. For more information, see P. Privett, 'Play', in A. Richards and P. Privett (eds.), *Through the Eyes of a Child: New Insights in Theology from a Child's Perspective* (London: Church House Publishing, 2009), pp. 101–127 (p. 105).

2. Godly Play is one of several variations of the Montessori tradition of religious education and has been developed in the United States by Dr Jerome Berryman. It invites listeners into stories and encourages them to connect the stories with personal experience. Children are welcomed into a 'sacred space', told a stylized story from the Bible and then encouraged to think about it with 'I wonder . . .' questions before responding in play and creative activities. For more information, see www.godlyplay.org.uk.

3. K. Ginsburg, 'The Importance of Play in Promoting Healthy Child Development and Maintaining Strong Parent-Child Bonds', *Pediatrics* 119 (2007), pp. 182–191.

4. In T. Hart, *The Secret Spiritual World of Children* (California: New World Library, 2003), p. xi.

184 | SLUGS AND SNAILS AND PUPPY DOGS' TAILS

5. For instance, Boulton (1998); Pellegrini (1988); Connor (1989); Costabile et al. (1991); Schafer and Smith (1996), all cited in P. Holland, *We Don't Play with Guns Here: War, Weapon and Superhero Play in the Early Years* (Maidenhead: Open University Press, 2003).

6. Holland, *We Don't Play with Guns Here.*

7. J. W. Fowler, *Faithful Change: The Personal and Public Challenges of Postmodern Life* (Nashville: Abingdon Press, 1996), p. 46.

8. R. Nye, 'Spirituality', in Richards and Privett (eds.), *Through the Eyes of a Child*, pp. 68–84 (p. 69).

9. E. Jordan, 'Fighting Boys and Fantasy Play: The Construction of Masculinity in the Early Years of School', *Gender and Education* 7 (1) (1995), pp. 69–86 (p. 75).

10. M. W. Watson and Y. Peng, 'The Relations between Toy Gun Play and Children's Aggressive Behaviour', *Early Education and Development* 3 (4) (1992), pp. 370–389 (p. 370).

11. See the conclusions in J. L. Singer (ed.), *The Child's World of Make Believe: Experimental Studies of Imaginative Play* (New York: Academic Press, 1973).

12. 'The lessons the scholars learn from one another in the playground are worth a hundred fold more than what they learn in the classroom'; Rousseau, *Emile* (1762), cited in G. Redmond, 'The First Tom Brown's Schooldays: Origins and Evolution of "Muscular Christianity" in Children's Literature', *Quest* 30 (1978), pp. 4–18.

13. N. J. Watson, S. Weir and S. Friend, 'The Development of Muscular Christianity in Victorian Britain and Beyond', *Journal of Religion and Society* 7 (2005), accessed online, http://moses.creighton.edu/JRS/.

14. Cited in ibid.

15. S. Frosh, A. Phoenix and R. Pattman, *Young Masculinities: Understanding Boys in Contemporary Society* (Basingstoke: Palgrave Macmillan, 2001), pp. 10–12.

16. There are various online resources and agencies attempting to use football as a vehicle for evangelism. Check out http://www.ycfl.org.uk and the Ambassadors in Sport website, http://www.aisint.org/.

17. Privett, 'Play', in Richards and Privett (eds.), *Through the Eyes of a Child*, pp. 101–127 (p. 117).

18. 'Tag Rugby is a fun and exciting form of non-contact rugby suitable for males and females of all ages and abilities. There are no scrums and line-outs and tackling is not allowed. It can be played as a family fun game in the local park or on the beach with teams comprising of as few as 4 or 5 players, or as a competitive 7-a-side game in organised leagues and festivals.' See www.tagrugby.co.uk.

3. Once upon a time

1. J.-P. Sartre, *Les Mots*, or *Words*, tr. Irene Clephane, new ed. (London: Penguin, 2000).
2. See the work of C. Erricker, J. Erricker, D. Sullivan, C. Ota and M. Fletcher, *The Education of the Whole Child* (London: Cassell, 1997); and D. Hay and R. Nye, *Spirit of the Child* (London: HarperCollins, 1998).
3. H. Anderson and E. Foley, *Mighty Stories, Dangerous Rituals: Weaving Together the Human and the Divine* (San Francisco: Jossey-Bass, 2001), p. 57.
4. E. Havelock, 'The Coming of Literate Communication to Western Culture', *Journal of Communication* (Winter 1980), p. 91.
5. For a discussion on the causes of this and some possible solutions, read G. Moss, *Literacy and Gender: Researching Texts, Contexts and Readers* (Abingdon: Routledge, 2007).
6. J. W. Berryman, *Godly Play: An Imaginative Approach to Religious Education* (Minneapolis: Augsburg Fortress, 1995), p. 64.
7. See Matthew 7:24–27; Luke 6:46–49.
8. M. Yaconelli, *Dangerous Wonder: The Adventure of a Childlike Faith* (Colorado Springs: NavPress, 1998).
9. See, for instance, B. Bettelheim, *The Uses of Enchantment: The Meaning and Importance of Fairy Tales* (London: Penguin, 1991).
10. See, for instance, Anderson and Foley, *Mighty Stories, Dangerous Rituals*, p. xiii; P. Ballard and J. Pritchard, *Practical Theology in Action* (London: SPCK, 1996), p. 128; D. McAdams, *The Stories We Live By: Personal Myths and the Making of the Self* (New York: Morrow, 1993), p. 27.
11. D. I. Smith and J. Shortt, *The Bible and the Task of Teaching It* (Nottingham: The Stapleford Centre, 2002), p. 21.
12. P. O'Connell Killen and J. De Beer, *The Art of Theological Reflection* (New York: The Crossroad Publishing Company, 1999), p. 24.
13. G. Wolff Pritchard, *Offering the Gospel to Children* (Cambridge, USA: Cowley Publications, 1992).
14. Attention Deficit Hyperactivity Disorder.
15. Written by Max Lucado and published by Crossway Books, USA.
16. M. Yaconelli, *Contemplative Youth Ministry: Practising the Presence of Jesus with Young People* (London: SPCK, 2006).
17. K. Haven, *Story Proof: The Science behind the Startling Power of Story* (Santa Barbara: Libraries Unlimited, 2007), pp. 13–14.
18. ibid., p. 79.
19. See, for instance, D. Maclaren, *Mission Implausible: Restoring Credibility to the Church* (Milton Keynes: Paternoster Press, 2004), p. 114; and a

report from Yorkshire and Humber Assembly in 2002 entitled 'Religious Literacy', which comments that 'religious literacy is at a very low level', cited in L. Barley, *Christian Roots, Contemporary Spirituality* (London: Church House Publishing, 2006), p. 18.

4. Make it go away

1. R. Coles, *The Spiritual Life of Children* (London: HarperCollins, 1992).
2. K. Adams, B. Hyde and R. Woolley, *The Spiritual Dimension of Childhood* (London: Jessica Kingsley Publishers, 2008), p. 36.
3. Obsessive Compulsive Disorders. Visible compulsions include such actions as checking, cleaning or avoidance. Less visible OCD compulsions can be as simple as repeatedly humming tunes, counting in your head or playing subconscious word games.
4. See, for instance, Ian Adams's book on modern monasticism, *Cave Refectory Road: Monastic Rhythms for Contemporary Living* (Norwich: Canterbury Press, 2010).
5. For resources, and contact details for local support groups, see www.childbereavement.org.uk, and www.crusebereavementcare.org.uk.

5. Poo, bum, willy

1. J. Millar, 'Nourishing the Inner Life', seminar at the International Conference on Children's Spirituality, Ballarat, Australia, January 2008 (notes taken by Ruth Wills).
2. S. Frosh, A. Phoenix and R. Pattman, *Young Masculinities: Understanding Boys in Contemporary Society* (Basingstoke: Palgrave Macmillan, 2001).
3. P. McGhee, *Understanding and Promoting the Development of Children's Humor* (Dubuque: Kendall Hunt, 2002).
4. S. Aamodt and S. Wang, *Welcome to Your Brain: The Science of Jet Lag, Love and Other Curiosities of Life* (London: Rider, 2008), p. 105.

6. Rock and paper and scissors

1. K. Adams, B. Hyde and R. Woolley, *The Spiritual Dimension of Childhood* (London: Jessica Kingsley Publishers, 2008), p. 73.
2. F. L. Shults and S. J. Sandage, *Transforming Spirituality: Integrating Theology and Psychology* (Grand Rapids: Baker Academic, 2006), p. 131.
3. H. Gardner, *Art, Mind and Brain: A Cognitive Approach to Creativity* (New York: Basic Books, 1984), pp. 87–89.
4. These were: *Last Supper*, Margaret Ackland, 1996, Australia; *Peace Be Still*, He Qi, 1998, China; *The Baptism of Jesus Christ*, Pheoris West, 1992, North America; *Jesus Washing the Disciples' Feet*, Dinah Roe

Kendall, 1996, UK; *The Risen Christ Reveals Himself First to the Two Women*, George Nene, 1998, Zimbabwe; *The Agony in the Garden*, Giovanni Bellini, © National Gallery Company Ltd, 2000; *The Supper at Emmaus*, Michelangelo Merisi da Caravaggio, © National Gallery Company Ltd, 2000.

5. T. Eaude, 'Do Young Boys and Girls Have Distinct and Different Approaches and Needs in Relation to Spiritual Development?', *International Journal of Children's Spirituality* 9 (1) (April 2004), pp. 53–65 (p. 64).

6. L. Sweet, *Soul Tsunami: Sink or Swim in New Millennium Culture* (Grand Rapids: Zondervan, 1999).

7. T. Graves, 'The Pragmatic-Participatory Model', in M. J. Anthony (ed.), *Perspectives on Children's Spiritual Formation: Four Views* (Tennessee: Broadman & Holman Publishers, 2006), pp. 165–224 (p. 184).

8. Luke 22:41; Ephesians 3:14.

9. Matthew 26:39; Mark 14:35; 1 Corinthians 14:25.

10. Mark 11:25; Luke 18:11, 13; 1 Timothy 2:8.

11. J. M. Twenge, 'The Multifactorial Approach and Organization of Gender-Related Attributes', *Psychology of Women Quarterly* 23 (1999), pp. 485–502.

12. See www.thebricktestament.com.

7. Pauses and ponderings

1. S. Teasdale, 'Thoughts', *The Collected Poems* (Macmillan, 1937).

2. L. S. Allen, M. F. Richey, Y. M. Chai and R. A. Gorski, 'Sex Differences in the Corpus Callosum of the Living Human Being', *Journal of Neuroscience* 11 (1991), pp. 933–942.

3. D. Hay and R. Nye, *Spirit of the Child* (London: Harper Collins, 1998), p. 16.

4. S. May, 'The Contemplative-Reflective Model', in M. J. Anthony (ed.), *Perspectives on Children's Spiritual Formation: Four Views* (Tennessee: Broadman & Holman Publishers, 2006).

5. T. Eaude, 'Do Young Boys and Girls Have Distinct and Different Approaches and Needs in Relation to Spiritual Development?', *International Journal of Children's Spirituality* 9 (1) (April 2004), pp. 53–65 (p. 64).

6. P. O'Connell Killen and J. De Beer, *The Art of Theological Reflection* (New York: The Crossroad Publishing Company, 1999), p. 20.

7. Luke 2:52.

8. B. D. McLaren, *More Ready Than You Realize: The Power of Everyday Conversations* (Michigan: Zondervan, 2002, repr. 2006), p. 74.

9. Deuteronomy 11:19.

10. N. Lamm, *The Shema: Spirituality and Law in Judaism as Exemplified in the Shema, the Most Important Passage in the Torah* (Philadelphia: Jewish Publication Society, 1998), p. 159.

11. A. Shier-Jones (ed.), *Children of God: Towards a Theology of Childhood* (Peterborough: Epworth, 2007), p. 68.

12. S. Frosh, A. Phoenix and R. Pattman, *Young Masculinities: Understanding Boys in Contemporary Society* (Basingstoke: Palgrave Macmillan, 2001), p. 16.

13. S. Biddulph, *Raising Boys* (London: Thorsons, 1997), pp. 40–41.

14. www.autism.org.uk/nas/jsp/polopoly.jsp?d=1049&a=3370, accessed 4 June 2009.

15. Polanyi, cited in J. W. Fowler, *Faithful Change: The Personal and Public Challenges of Postmodern Life* (Nashville: Abingdon Press, 1996), p. 40.

16. L. Barley, *Christian Roots, Contemporary Spirituality* (London: Church House Publishing, 2006), p. 41.

17. 'Beliefs and Morals', a Populus national survey for the *Sun*, published in June 2005, suggested that 65% of the adults in Britain said that they prayed.

18. D. Long, D. Elkind and B. Spilka, 'The Child's Conception of Prayer', *Journal of Scientific Study of Religion* 6 (1967), pp. 101–109.

19. T. Holmes, 'Teaching Children the Art of Prayer and Contemplation', *The Times*, 2 October 2004.

20. D. Hay, *Something There: The Biology of the Human Spirit* (London: Darton, Longman and Todd, 2006).

21. 'Results suggest that weekly public religious activity was significantly associated with better health and well-being. Furthermore, this relationship was stronger for men than for women and was influenced by denominational affiliation. When public religious activity, private religious activity, and spiritual experiences were considered simultaneously, public religious activity emerged as the most consistent predictor of health and well-being among men.' From J. Maselko and L. D. Kubzansky, 'Gender Differences in Religious Practices, Spiritual Experiences and Health: Results from the US General Social Survey', *Social Sciences and Medicine* 62 (2006), pp. 2848–2860.

22. I have found R. J. Foster, *Celebration of Discipline* (London: Hodder & Stoughton, new ed. 2008) very helpful in this regard.

23. See http://ignatianspirituality.com/ignatian-prayer/the-examen.

8. The eleventh commandment

1. F. Buechner, *Listening to Your Life* (San Francisco: HarperCollins, 1992), p. 182.

2. G. Gutiérrez, *We Drink from Our Own Wells: The Spiritual Journey of a People*, 20th anniversary ed. (Maryknoll: Orbis, 2003), p. 31.

3. T. Hart, *The Secret Spiritual World of Children* (California: New World Library, 2003), p. 59.

4. K. White, 'Creation', in A. Richards and P. Privett (eds.), *Through the Eyes of a Child: New Insights in Theology from a Child's Perspective* (London: Church House Publishing, 2009), pp. 44–67.

5. Korczak, cited in K. Copsey, *From the Ground Up: Understanding the Spiritual World of the Child* (Oxford: Bible Reading Fellowship, 2005), p. 29.

6. D. Smith, *Making Sense of Spiritual Development* (Nottingham: The Stapleford Centre, 1999), p. 15.

7. D. Hay and R. Nye, *Spirit of the Child* (London: HarperCollins, 1998), pp. 17–18.

8. See http://faculty.plts.edu/qpence/html/kohlberg.htm, accessed 18 January 2009.

9. J. Watson, 'Preparing Spirituality for Citizenship', *International Journal for Children's Spirituality* 8 (1) (2003), pp. 9–24 (p. 19).

10. B. Moss, *Religion and Spirituality* (Lyme Regis: Russell House Publishing, 2005), p. 12.

11. Scripture Union partnered with A Rocha, a Christian nature conservation organization, to produce Wastewatchers, a five-day holiday club for five- to eleven-year-olds, especially suitable for children who are not yet part of a church community.

12. The National Advisory Committee on Creative and Cultural Education was established in 1998 to make recommendations to the then Secretary of State for Education and Employment and Secretary of State for Culture, Media and Sport 'on the creative and cultural development of young people through formal and informal education: to take stock of current provision and to make proposals for principles, policies and practice'. The committee was chaired by Professor Ken Robinson and its report was published in 1999.

9. Thrills and spills

1. Story told by Simon Wells, mountaineering instructor.

2. V. Madge, *Children in Search of Meaning* (London: SCM Press, 1969), p. 107.

3. D. Gardner, *Risk: The Science and Politics of Fear* (London: Virgin Books, 2009), p. 14.

4. S. Aamodt and S. Wang, *Welcome to Your Brain: The Science of Jet Lag, Love and Other Curiosities of Life* (London: Rider, 2008).

5. J. Lindon, *Too Safe for Their Own Good?* (London: National Early Years Network, 1999).

6. *Every Child Matters* (Department for Education and Skills, 2003), p. 6.

7. R. Layard and J. Dunn, *A Good Childhood: Searching for Values in a Competitive Age* (London: Penguin, 2009).

8. See Mills (2001) and Woolley (2007), cited in K. Adams, B. Hyde and R. Woolley, *The Spiritual Dimension of Childhood* (London: Jessica Kingsley Publishers, 2008), p. 49.

9. K. White, 'Creation', in A. Richards and P. Privett (eds.), *Through the Eyes of a Child: New Insights in Theology from a Child's Perspective* (London: Church House Publishing, 2009), pp. 44–67 (p. 55).

10. I game, therefore I am

1. www.cartoonstock.com.

2. See www.childwise.co.uk for up-to-date research data on multimedia trends amongst children.

3. See Matthew 5 and John 17:16.

4. This is the central theme of Neil Postman's book, *The Disappearance of Childhood* (New York: Vintage Books, 1996).

5. C. Jenks, *Childhood* (London: Routledge, 1996).

6. T. Gill, *No Fear: Growing Up in a Risk Averse Society* (London: Calouste Gulbenkian Foundation, 2007).

7. See M. Hillman, J. Adams and J. Whitelegg, *One False Move: A Study of Children's Independent Mobility* (London: Policy Studies Institute, 1993); and R. Wheway and A. Millward, *Child's Play: Facilitating Play on Housing Estates* (London: Chartered Institute of Housing, 1997).

8. S. Jeffries, 'Is Television Destroying Our Children's Minds?', *Guardian*, Wednesday 21 July 2004.

9. Quoted from the ChildWise report by Lucy Ward, 'Life through a Lens: How Britain's Children Eat, Sleep and Breathe TV', *Guardian*, Wednesday 16 January 2008.

10. See Postman, *The Disappearance of Childhood*, p. 78.

11. See, for instance, L. S. Allen and R. A. Gorski, 'Sexual Dimorphism of the Anterior Commissure and Massa Intermedia of the Human Brain', *The Journal of Comparative Neurology* 312 (1) (1 October 1991), pp. 97–104.

12. A. Kohn, *Punished by Rewards* (Boston: Houghton Mifflin, 1993).

13. J. W. Fowler, *Faithful Change: The Personal and Public Challenges of Postmodern Life* (Nashville: Abingdon Press, 1996), p. 111.

14. A CBBC programme based on a series of books about children in care, written by Jacqueline Wilson.

15. A feature-length cartoon film about zoo animals that escape, made by Dreamworks.

Go and do likewise

1. F. Brown, *Play Theories and the Value of Play* (Library and Information Service, National Children's Bureau, 2006).

Appendix 1

1. T. Eaude, 'Do Young Boys and Girls Have Distinct and Different Approaches and Needs in Relation to Spiritual Development?', *International Journal of Children's Spirituality* 9 (1) (April 2004), pp. 53–65 (p. 57).
2. See www.statistics.gov.uk.
3. ibid.
4. See www.nas.org.uk.
5. ibid.
6. See www.homeoffice.gov.uk.

Appendix 2

1. I came across the Tellegen scale in Tanya Luhrmann's brilliant chapter in J. A. Schaler (ed.), *Howard Gardner Under Fire* (Chicago: Open Court Publishing Co., 2006). Luhrmann has done a great deal of research into different spiritual expressions or experiences including 'white magic' and charismatic Christianity. She felt, of all the measures that she used, that the Tellegen scale was the most effective in identifying people who had unusual, intense spiritual experiences.
2. M. Frost and A. Hirsch, *The Shaping of Things to Come* (Massachusetts: Hendrickson Publishers Inc., 2003).
3. G. Davies, 'What is Spiritual Development? Primary Head Teachers' Views', *International Journal of Children's Spirituality* 3 (2) (December 1993).
4. G. Thomas, *Sacred Pathways* (Grand Rapids: Zondervan, 2002).

Appendix 3

1. X:site is an event run in partnership with local churches and supported by Scripture Union. The events are for children aged between seven and eleven and, together with enthusiastic volunteers, they pack games, videos, dramas and music into a fast-moving evening to help children learn more about Jesus. For more information, visit www.xsite.org.
2. See, for instance, Tamminen (1991) and Francis (1987), cited in D. Hay and R. Nye, *Spirit of the Child* (London: HarperCollins, 1998), p. 49.

3. D. Hay, *Something There: The Biology of the Human Spirit* (London: Darton, Longman and Todd, 2006), p. 128.

4. 'The spiritual and moral development of pupils implies the need for a variety of learning experiences which provide opportunities for pupils to:
    - discuss matters of personal concern;
    - develop relationships with adults and peers;
    - develop a sense of belonging to a community;
    - be challenged by exploring the beliefs and values of others while deepening their knowledge and understanding of their own faith or beliefs;
    - discuss religious and philosophical questions;
    - understand why people reach certain decisions on spiritual and moral issues, and how those decisions affect their lives;
    - experience what is aesthetically challenging;
    - experience silence and reflection.'

    SCAA Discussion Paper: No. 3 – Spiritual and Moral Development (September 1995).

5. Trevor and Margaret Cooling have produced some fantastic resources for using fine art in the classroom, published by the Stapleford Centre.